The Road To
AMBRIDGE

June Spencer

The Road To
AMBRIDGE

My life, Peggy & *The Archers*

JR
BOOKS

First published in Great Britain in 2010 by
JR Books, 10 Greenland Street, London NW1 0ND
www.jrbooks.com

A catalogue record for this book is available from the British Library.

ISBN 978-1-907532-25-2

1 3 5 7 9 10 8 6 4 2

Printed by Clays Ltd, St Ives plc

Contents

Acknowledgements

Huge thanks to Ros Parker-Ives, who suggested I should write my memoirs and then found herself lumbered with the job of deciphering my long-hand scrawl and typing it. To my daughter Roz for her love and support and for jogging my memory on occasion. To *The Archers'* editor Vanessa Whitburn for her enthusiastic encouragement from the outset. To Lesley Wilson for her cheerful expertise in guiding me through the difficult job of editing, and last but not least to Jeremy Robson for amazingly having faith in me. My deep gratitude to you all.

Chapter 1

Beginnings

'You're going to be in *The Archers*, aren't you?'

'Am I?' I said, 'What are *The Archers*?'

It was in the spring of 1950 and I was rehearsing a radio play in the Birmingham Studios when another actress posed that question to me. I never realised then that *The Archers* was to become such a big part of my life for the next 60 years – and still going! Looking back, I can see how so many things in my childhood pointed the way to a career in acting and how fate took a hand in leading me through the theatre into radio and thence to *The Archers*, with Peggy becoming my alter ego.

But I was a busy radio actress long before then. My first broadcast was in November 1943 when I was cast in a 15-minute programme called *Railways in Wartime*. Blockbuster, it was not! Being young and keen, I arrived at the BBC Midland Region to find the studio in darkness. I fumbled about and found a switch – it wasn't the light, it was the fire alarm! Mayhem ensued, but at least the world of radio knew I had arrived. I suppose I should start at the beginning, though.

I was born on 14 June 1919 in Sherwood, Nottingham – Robin Hood country. My parents were known as 'the young couple with the pretty baby' – I quote my mother. In fact, before I was two, I came second in a baby beauty competition on stage in Rhyl, where we were on holiday. My prize was what I proudly referred to as 'my wife and fork for being a good girl.' More importantly, I can clearly remember being on stage and facing an impenetrable wall of light as I danced my dolly, as instructed by my mother. Perhaps this was when the acting bug first bit me.

These days, it seems to be the thing to start one's life-story by describing a deprived or abused childhood, but I can't do that. I was greatly loved and if anything, over-cosseted – I was a happy child. Don't run away with the idea that an only child is a spoilt one, though – it works both ways – but I only came to realise that much later on.

I was born at home, apparently with great difficulty, which involved my father having to mount his bicycle and pedal like mad for the doctor as I was more than the midwife could cope with. It seems I put her off the job for years and the reason why I was an only child was that my father insisted he was not going through that again.

My father was one of seven. His father had a tailoring business but both he and my grandmother died before I was born. I know nothing of their forebears. My mother, on the other hand, was the second eldest of nine and I learnt more about my family background from her. Grandfather Thorne – the only grand-parent I knew – was a country boy who ran away to join the East Surrey Regiment. He served in India and when he returned to England as the Colonel's batman, he fell in love with the children's nanny. Isobel James was 19 and her parents did not approve of the 26-year-old Frederick – her sisters had made much better matches. And so they eloped from Hythe to – for some reason – Nottingham. There he worked, first as a miner and then a surface worker, and they raised nine children. When she was only 39 Isobel contracted appendicitis and after refusing to have the then quite new operation, it became peritonitis and so she died. Grandfather, meanwhile, lived to 94.

What a marvellous old chap he was. I can remember sitting on his knee and twirling the ends of his military moustache. He was a great walker, tramping for miles with his dog Prince to visit various sons and daughters. A keen gardener, he grew vegetables on his own allotment. He once complained when he was 90 that it was getting all too much for him. His son said: 'Well, Dad, you're not as young as you used to be,' to which Grandad replied: 'No – I mean I'm growing more than we can eat!'

I was in close contact with all my uncles and aunts except for Uncle Billy, a very talented golf pro who was killed in the First World War. He died in action during the terrible battle of the Somme and it was at Beaumont Hamel that he died. The wonderful novel *Birdsong* by Sebastian Faulks describes the action so vividly and brought home to me the circumstances of his death so poignantly – I wish I had known him.

Of the rest of the boys one became a captain in the First World War, one was a publican, another company secretary to Milletts and the two youngest achieved their hearts' desires and became engine drivers. The youngest, Reginald, was born on Trafalgar Day so his middle name was Nelson. Incidentally, I've always thought that great hero has been much maligned over the years. I don't believe he said, 'Kiss me, Hardy' as he lay dying; it's far more likely that he was saying, 'Kismet, Hardy' – fate!

We also had a family hero. My great, great grandfather Jarvist Arnold was a Trinity House pilot and also Coxswain of the Kingsdown lifeboat. There were no high-powered engines in those days – instead they would put to sea under sail in terrible storms or row to rescue ships wrecked on the Goodwins. To quote a poem written after the epic rescue of the crew of the *Sorrento* in 1872:

> God bless the lifeboat and its crew,
>> Its coxswain stout and bold,
> And Jarvist Arnold is his name,
>> Sprung from the Vikings old,
> Who made the waves and winds their slaves,
>> As likewise we do so,
> Whilst still Britannia rules the waves,
> And the stormy winds do blow;
> And the old Cork Float that safety brought,
>> We'll hold in honour leal,
> And it shall grace the chiefest place,
>> In Kingsdown, hard by Deal.

He looks such a jolly old boy in his photograph and so like my Uncle Reg who, after losing his third wife when in his eighties, declared: 'I'm not going to get married again – I'm just going to enjoy myself!' But I digress . . .

The house where I was eventually born and lived for the first seven years of my life was a pleasant rented semi-detached with three floors and cellars. Its tiled hall contained a mahogany hallstand and chair. The drawing room had a piano and three-piece suite in grey corded-velvet, while the dining room held a large table with a chenille cloth and huge mahogany sideboard. There was also a butler's pantry where my father made his own ginger beer which exploded one night, whereupon he bravely went downstairs to confront what he thought were armed intruders. Opposite was the door to the cellars: one for coal, another stored wine and one was used as a general dump. The big cosy kitchen had a black-leaded grate and beyond was the large scullery, which nowadays would be called the utility room. It contained a fire-heated copper, the predecessor of a washing machine. My first sight of snowflakes was through the high-up window of that same kitchen and the wonder of it has stayed with me to this day.

On the first floor were three bedrooms, one of which was a day nursery for me. My mother had worked as a nurse to a wealthy family in London so I had the benefit of her experience! There was a walk-in linen cupboard, a bathroom and a lavatory. On the top floor were two more rooms, one of which was a bedroom for our little country maid. No electricity – the house was lit by gas.

Looking back, I realise how lucky I was to have a playroom all to myself. The carpet was green and white, the dado of seaside scenes. Best of all was Bubbles: my rocking horse, with a real horsehair mane and tail and red leather harness. I can clearly recall the awful taste of the leather when I sucked it. The miles I rode on him! What marvellous adventures we shared in my fertile imagination.

Sometimes I had the company of the boy next door, but he wasn't so keen after I nearly strangled him because he wouldn't give up my favourite toy. His cry for help brought my mother rushing up the stairs: 'Mrs Spencer, Mrs Spencer, look what she's doing to me!' Many years later I heard that he had at one time been aide-de-camp to the Governor of the Bahamas.

Each day the milkman called, driving a little horse-drawn chariot like Ben Hur's, on which were placed huge cans of milk. They were measured out in dippers into one's own jug. Sometimes, at no older than six, I would be sent off with a jug to the dairy in nearby Carrington marketplace to buy six penny-worth of cream, which would be whipped to form a thick layer on a huge sherry trifle.

When I was three my young Auntie Win (who I adored) was visiting us. I wanted to go with her to the shops, but I was told that I couldn't. 'No' was not a word I recognised and so I pushed the hall chair up to the door, climbed up to open it and I was away. On reaching the shops, I was soon taken up by a little crowd of urchins, who took me down a path past some back gardens, telling a woman en route, 'Look what we've found!'

Rejoining the main road, I was grabbed by my distraught father, who clasped me to him in relief – upon which, they told me, I kicked him smartly in the stomach, yelling: 'I want to stay and play with my little flends!' What safe and harmless days they were then.

Poor Daddy, he deserved better. It was he who would come and sit by me and sing me to sleep whenever I lay awake at night. 'I'm Forever Blowing Bubbles' was a favourite and 'I Passed By Your Window When the Morning Was Red' (or bread, as I sang).

My life has always been filled with music. Of course in those days there was no television and radio was in its infancy. People made their own music. Almost everyone could either sing or play an instrument, often both. My parents both had pleasing singing voices and Mother was also a very good mandolin player.

My mother would have made a perfect 'soubrette' being pretty, slim and dainty. In addition to her light singing voice she might have been a dancer, being loose-limbed. She could do the splits and was still able to perform high kicks into her eighties, especially at Christmas time after a glass of bubbly. Much later, I learnt from relatives that she would have loved to have gone on the stage, which I find hard to reconcile with the fact that she did everything she could to stop me! When I finally made it, she said: 'Oh well, I suppose it was meant' and thereafter became my sternest critic.

I would hear the gathering of their friends as I lay in bed and would drift off to sleep to the sounds of 'Shipmates O' Mine' (Father) and 'Where My Caravan Has Rested (Mother). The piano was played by one of the guests and accompanied by the syncopation of a young man's banjo. There would be a break for supper and on one occasion disaster struck.

In the dining room was a brass standard lamp and it was fuelled by oil. While the party had been enjoying the singsong, the lamp exuded black, sooty smoke and everything, including the sherry trifle with its thick layer of cream bristling with almonds, cherries and angelica, was totally ruined. If only clingfilm had been invented!

I started music lessons at the age of five and at six I was playing little tunes and singing the accompanying words. Lessons continued until I was 16 and passed the Advanced Associated Board Exam but it was a hard slog for my small hands – I was not cut out to be a pianist.

The arrival of the gramophone was a red-letter day. A large packing case from London was opened in the garden and there it was: a square, light oak box on turned legs, with a shelf at the bottom for storing records. It was a wind-up one, of course. There were two little doors at the front and opening or closing them controlled the volume. It gave us years of pleasure. Now I could go off to sleep to the sound of 'In a Monastery Garden' or the overture to *Tannhauser* and much later Richard Tauber singing 'You Are My Heart's Delight'. Later still, I would shut myself in with it and dance to the pop tunes of the day.

Some of us may not like the lyrics of today's music but I have to confess some of the songs of my young days were pretty silly, too. 'Yes, We Have No Bananas, We Have No Bananas Today' was one. Another was 'Ain't She Sweet, She's Coming Down the Street' which to certain small boys became: 'Ain't She Sweet, She's Stuck to the Lavatory Seat'.

My introduction to stage lighting in Rhyl soon led me again to the stage – or rather onto a natural stage in the garden of a drama teacher. At exactly three years old, I was cast as 'King of the Land of Nod' at the school's annual display. The backdrop of moon and stars was in a natural cave, part of Nottingham Castle Rock, and I was seated on a draped form with a tiny attendant either end. I remember one of them looked to me as if she might fall off and so I considerately changed places with her. This caused a problem, which had to be sorted in full view of the audience.

Soon my cue came and a whisper told me to make my entrance, clutching my handful of magic stardust. The leading lady, aged 12, said: 'He never speaks, he only smiles!' Upon which, having scanned my audience, I said loudly: 'Oh look – there's Daddy!' This got a good laugh and I received an even bigger laugh a moment later with, 'Oh Mummy, it's raining!' Clearly, this reception went to my head for ever since I've liked nothing better than making people laugh.

Looking back over 91 years I have a kaleidoscope of memories. They give me glimpses of the world I used to know and sometimes a scent or sound triggers a memory of when I was very young, such as the smell of coal dust as the coal men tipped sacks of coal through the manhole outside in the pavement, which went straight into the cellar under our house.

I remember going shopping with my mother and my favourite shop was always the Maypole Dairy. The tiled floor was spread with sawdust, chairs for the customers set by the counters and huge blocks of butter expertly carved off with wooden butter pats, shaped up and wrapped in greaseproof paper. I loved the dairy smell. All produce was weighed and then packaged: biscuits, coffee, lard . . . all sold 'loose'. No wonder children in those days loved playing 'shops'.

I soon had a tricycle and as our home was on a small hill, I could get up a good turn of speed freewheeling down it. Going round the corner at the bottom, I showed off my driving skills by putting my hand out. It was pointed out to me that as I was turning to the right it should be the right hand, not the left, as I always did. Well, I needed my right hand for steering, didn't I? In time I graduated to a Fairy Cycle (a child's bicycle) and then a bigger one. I was refused a bicycle on the grounds that it was 'too dangerous' so I used to ride a friend's bike, which was far too big for me.

My hair has always been as straight as two sticks but that wouldn't do for Mother. Every night I suffered the dreaded curl rags. Each section of hair rolled up in a rag and then the beastly tug as they were tied. I was glad when school started and my hair was 'bobbed'.

Supper was always a bowl of brown bread and milk with a spoonful of golden syrup. If I'm feeling under the weather I sometimes have it even now – and with the same old spoon from so long ago. Comfort food!

The lengths that I would go to in order to do a bit of 'acting'! At about four years old I walked round the block to the main road and accosted two ladies. I remember gazing up at them and saying, 'Please can you tell me the way to Bingham Road [where I lived]?' After they had bent over and pointed out the way to go, I thanked them. As they walked away, they turned round and gave me amused glances. I guess they knew I was pretending – even with only myself as an audience I was a compulsive 'ham'.

Lying in bed the night before my thirteenth birthday I told myself, 'I shall never be twelve again (tearfully). And it's been so lovely being twelve' and then, 'Of course I'm only acting.'

A cafe of any size in those days would have a small orchestra, so to go out to tea was quite an event. While enjoying tea and rich cakes you listened to popular tunes from the current musical comedies and operettas plus other light classical music. The theatres too had their own orchestras and so there was plenty of work for musicians. Even our little rep theatre had its trio of piano, violin and cello. I remember sitting on the stage during an interval in *Ladies in Retirement* when I enjoyed listening to the 'Warsaw Concerto' being expertly played. Now all we get is canned music!

Children these days are so lucky in the comfort of their casual clothes. I was stuffed into Chilprufe underwear, on top of which was the dreaded liberty bodice from the buttons of which were suspenders ending in black woollen stockings and topped by navy gym knickers. How I pleaded to be allowed to take those stockings off at the first warm rays of spring, but Mother would say, 'Ne'er cast a clout till May be out' – and she meant the month, not the bush. And if I whined her into submission and was allowed to take them off – oh, the bliss of air on bare legs! Believe me, it was one of the great experiences of life after a long, hard winter.

We had a holiday on a farm when I was very young. I can clearly remember the delicious scent of bacon and mushrooms frying in the farmhouse kitchen. I loved the smell, but the sight of those black things in the pan really put me off! Now I love mushrooms.

I don't remember the following incident but it shows certain inventiveness. Apparently the farmer's wife told me that I could have any apples I found under the bush on the ground. One day I came in with a very nice apple, which surprised her as she had just gathered up all the fallen ones. I insisted that I had picked it up off the ground. In the end I admitted that I had pulled it off the bush, put it on the ground – and then picked it up off the ground as instructed. You have to admit it was a nice try!

I was never awfully keen on dolls. My favourite toys were my teddy, monkey and golliwog – I hardly dare write the latter as it is strictly off-limits these days. Sad, because it was a favourite of so many children. When we took our son David to a big toyshop and gave him free rein to choose what he would like to celebrate his adoption day, he chose a golly.

My teddy bear survived into my twenties when he began to leak sawdust and had to go, but I have one big teddy and two small ones as replacements and they sit on the spare bed in my room. My monkey was also special and when a young cousin was coming to visit my parents were very surprised when I announced that I would give Peggy my monkey. They were not so astonished when a few minutes later I tearfully admitted: 'I don't want to give Peggy my monkey!' And so it was suggested I lend it to her instead.

I became interested in dolls when Margie Dolls were invented (I was 11 or 12). They had movable joints and could stand up – amazing! Backdrops were painted and different sets of clothes made for the pair of them and so they became part of what was to be one of my earliest stage sets.

Chapter 2

Transport and Childhood

My father was a commercial traveller for Crawford's Biscuits and off he would go on his bicycle with a heavy bag of samples on each handlebar, sometimes taking the train to different parts of his area. I grew up surrounded by all the latest kinds of biscuits with the result that it was years before I thought of buying – or indeed wanting any.

To my father salesmanship was a science and he put his early experience to good use in later years as a lecturer on Salesmanship & Sales Management. When I was three, he bought a motorbike and sidecar. The sidecar was open to the elements and whenever it rained, Mother (with me on her knee) would hold a waterproof sheet over us. How her arms must have ached! However, we were off in all weathers and once got as far as London (120 miles) in heavy snow.

Before I was born, my mother had a rather frightening experience with a previous motorbike and sidecar owned by

Father. This apparently had a wickerwork sidecar and on one trip to the countryside a smell of burning was detected. Mother was just able to disembark before the sidecar burst into flames!

When I was six we had our first car. It was a second-hand baby Austin with its AA badge gleaming on the bonnet and I would proudly return the salute that all AA members received from the patrolman in those days. Our next car was a large second-hand open Standard tourer. The spare wheel was carried on the running board and on one occasion hadn't been properly strapped on. It came loose and we suddenly realised that it was bouncing merrily along the road in pursuit of us.

Father taught me to drive when I was 12. This was before the days of driving tests but of course I was under-age and uninsured. The roads were very quiet, especially on Sunday mornings when we would set off, my pigtails hidden inside my coat, and I would be instructed in three-point turns and hill starts. Father also taught me how to drive through water – bottom gear, lots of gas and slip the clutch. I've found this very useful in these days of floods! Eventually my lessons came to an abrupt end when Father learned that one of his friends had got in trouble for teaching his schoolboy son.

The moment when I was old enough to have a provisional driving licence I was back in the driving seat. By then tests had come into force but I failed the first time – for exceeding the speed limit! Over-confident, I expect. I passed the second time.

The first car I ever owned was a 1934 Standard 12, which had been laid up all through the war. She was a stately old girl, so I called her 'Aggie'. I paid £110 and I sold her two years later for £120. Not bad. She took me to Birmingham when *The Archers* first started in January 1951. There was frozen snow on the roads and Aggie had no heating, so I drove with a hot-water bottle on my knees and a blanket over that.

Then there was 'the banger'. This was an ancient Morris Eight, inside which it snowed, even with the windows shut. In later years I took the children touring in the New Forest, much to my husband's consternation: it served us well and had the bonus that Ros, my little girl, wasn't car sick in it whereas she always was when travelling in Roger's far superior vehicle. Her brother David, senior by two and half years, never failed to observe at certain points on the road: 'That's where she was sick last time.' Not exactly helpful!

Another comparable car was Bugsy – the first one I owned in Menorca. A Fiat 600, she had been run into the ground as a hire car. Initially, we had a difference of opinion: I expected her to go up hills and she only reluctantly agreed. She had one big advantage, though – a hole in the floor that was very useful for sweeping out sand. However, to return to the days of the Austin Seven . . .

It was exciting to wake on a bright summer's morning and hear my father calling, 'Come on, get up – we're going to Chapel!' Not church chapel, but Chapel-St-Leonard's, with its sand hills and sea, not too far from Skegness. Skegness ('Skeggy' for short) was for the main summer holiday. Deck chairs behind a wind-break for Mum and Dad, a bucket and spade for me; also rides on Tommy, my favourite donkey. We stayed at Mrs Pollard's boarding house on the seafront – 'No buckets and spades in the house'.

At 'Sea View' there wasn't the luxury of an 'en-suite bathroom' – something we take for granted now. The first knock on the door heralded an early-morning cup of tea and half an hour or so later a large enamel jug of hot water was delivered for washing and shaving.

The highlight of every holiday was when I was allowed to stay up late to go to 'Clements' concert party. Walking through the gardens lit by coloured fairy lights to the theatre was the part I remember best. I must have seen some of the comedians who passed through Fred Clement's Concert Party and later became big stars in the thirties and forties, but all I can recall of the shows was a young man in pyjamas and dressing gown singing a sad little song called 'Three O'Clock In The Morning'. I was probably quite shocked that he should appear in public in his night attire.

It was while staying at Mrs Pollard's that I started a very bad case of whooping cough. My mother and I were allowed to move to an attic room, where I coughed my heart out, whooped and fought for breath. The doctor there was the father of Elizabeth Allan, a famous Hollywood film star of those days.

I had already done measles as soon as I had started school. My rash was first noticed while taking tea at the Trocadero in London. I was whisked home and put to bed in my parents' room and given a book with a picture of a pierrot on the cover and a clockwork trainset that didn't run too well on the bed. Each afternoon the blinds were drawn and I drowsed to sparrows cheeping in the eaves. Nowadays the sound vividly brings back that time to me – it's always been one I love.

After a while we began to holiday further afield and I have just two memories of a short stay at a hotel in Brighton. At a nearby table in the dining room sat an old gentleman with a long white beard. This was fascinating enough for a seven-year-old but it became even more interesting as he drank his tomato soup and the white beard gradually turned a bright red.

My father had brought along a fishing line, which he hoped to use from the shore. It entailed throwing the weighted hook as far as possible without letting go of the wooden frame. 'That's a good throw,' he observed – and then realised he'd let go of the whole thing. End of fishing trip!

A holiday in the more exotic Torquay resulted in a chance encounter with a cousin my mother had never met before. 'Bunny' Rowe was bandmaster on the *Queen Mary* and he and his band were doing a guest appearance concert. This led to Mother being reunited with her mother's sister who on seeing me for the first time, aged 12, tearfully pronounced: 'She's so like poor dear Belle!' This was my granny who had died, aged 39.

Other holidays were spent in Worthing, Folkestone and Hunstanton. I didn't take a trip abroad until after the war.

For as long as I can remember – and even before that – I had a dear friend called Helen. She was two years older and began talking to me when I was wheeled past her garden gate in my pram. As we grew up, we attended the same prep school, joined the Brownies together and then went on to high school. We became inseparable and we vowed we would always be friends. And so we were until her death, some 60 years later.

Off we would go to the sweetshop to buy dolly mixtures for a halfpenny. We always went to Mother Piper's little shop because she would accept farthings (a quarter of an old penny). 'You won't get many,' she used to say as she counted them out into a little square of tissue paper. Then there were the gob-stoppers: 'Ukulele lady's eyes' – or 'dookaloola lady's eyes', as I called them. They changed colour as you sucked them and naturally, it was necessary for us to keep sticking our tongues out to see how they changed.

On my way to the sweetshop I once passed a street singer. I gather they were frequent in my mother's youth and would often be given a penny 'to go in the next street' – they were not good singers as a rule! On this occasion I felt that I really ought to give him my penny but greed got the better of me and so I carried on to the shop. He was still there when I came back so as a sop to my conscience, I offered him a sweet. He looked rather surprised but accepted it just the same. At least it stopped him singing for a bit.

The Misses Keating, two elderly maiden ladies, owned Mountford House School and one – Miss Emma – was my first music teacher. When the elder Miss Keating died, two young, go-ahead teachers bought the school but I stayed on until I was nine – I loved it.

At that time I was passionately in love with a little boy called

Tommy. During dictation one day I noticed he'd misspelled the word 'pigeon'. In a whisper, I told him what it should be, but I was spotted and called to Miss Sutton's office. Gently she told me that even though it wasn't for my own benefit, I was still cheating. I was so ashamed that I burst into tears, whereupon she took me on her knee and comforted me. No wonder I loved that school! In the crazy world of today, I suppose her actions would have given her a criminal record. Poor Tommy died of tuberculosis in his early twenties.

One day after lessons, two of the boys organised a boxing match in the barn attached to the school. We were issued with entry tickets and advised to bring our attaché cases to sit on. One in leather gauntlets, the other fur-backed mittens, the two boys set about each other with a will. It was short but fierce and I was lost in admiration when one of the contestants spat blood into the cloakroom hand-basin. His name was Reggie Simpson and he later found fame as a test cricketer.

I was an early reader and by the age of six, I was reading Grimm's Fairy Tales – just the ones with a pencilled tick, which were considered not too frightening. I used to get really fed up when I was given a book suitable for extremely young children that I considered uninteresting.

As an only child I read a lot to fill the long periods of time on my own. My mother would say, 'You've always got your head in a book.' I would read by torchlight under the bedclothes and many a time I would hear her voice outside the loo door: 'Have you got a book in there, June?' Of course, I usually had – I still love to read in bed.

In today's world of radio and TV news it is hard to remember that in the 1920s we only had newspapers and so world and even local affairs could seem quite remote. I still remember a photograph in the newspaper of the funeral cortège of Queen Alexandra, the beautiful consort of Edward VII. That was in 1925.

My father was never one of those out of work and although he earned less than £400 a year at that time we lived a comfortable, while not luxurious, life. I knew nothing of the poverty endured by the unemployed – to me, the General Strike of 1926 meant that all sorts of people were operating the tramcars! Once over, the drivers and conductors all wore Sherwood green uniforms.

We were one of the early families to own a crystal set. This consisted of a little black box on top of which were a crystal and a small handle with a triangle of fine wire at the end, known as a cat's whisker. It was twiddled over the crystal until the local radio station was obtained and if you listened on headphones, you could pick up someone singing or Children's Hour. This contraption was wired up to a very high pole in the garden.

I was taken to the Theatre Royal to see Peter Pan. Afterwards I terrified my parents by launching myself off the kitchen table, all the while shouting: 'I flew!' *Lilac Time* came next and later *The Girl Friend*, delightfully parodied in recent times as *The Boy Friend*.

In the meantime, annual stage appearances continued through drama classes and dancing displays with my school of dancing and it was then that I received my first fan letter from an admirer. He wrote that I was 'very good as the fairy queen' – I was nine and he was 12.

By now, we had moved to a newly built house. We had our foot on the property ladder! It was a pretty little detached home in a quiet crescent on a big plot, which my parents quickly turned into a lovely garden. Father grew fruit and vegetables, Mother was in charge of the flowers and I had my own little plot –I've loved gardening ever since.

A swing was built for me and there was a summerhouse, which I made my own special domain: it became 'the clubhouse' when I started a club with six of my girl friends. Every Friday after school we met in summertime. Each week I produced a handwritten magazine containing 'The Editress's Letter', puzzles, a short story and a serial that never ended. How my schoolwork suffered!

Very soon I cottoned on to the realisation that I had the makings of a theatre company of my own. Long-suffering friends later told me that I was a martinet about learning lines and turning up for rehearsal. I wrote the plays – with, of course, the best part for me – and made all the costumes. Admission was charged for the performances and Dr Barnardo's received the takings of 12 shillings and sixpence in the first year and 21 shillings the following year.

The crescent saw practically no traffic and so we children played cricket with a lamppost for a wicket. As a girl, I was allowed to bowl underarm and was quite the demon bowler. If the bat missed the ball, I hit the wicket and many a disgruntled boy was out.

There was an occasion when I decided to bowl overarm for a change. I walked away and when I turned to make my run-up, there wasn't a child in sight. They had all taken cover in the nearest front garden!

One of the neighbourhood boys who rejoiced in the name of Herbert was a Robin Hood fanatic – whom he pronounced 'Yobbin Hood'. His band of merry men were rather a tough lot, but he felt things were incomplete until he had a Maid Marion of his own and I found that I had been cast in the role. To play Maid Marion was an offer I couldn't refuse. However, the idea did not meet with the approval of the rest of the boys and they would only agree if I fulfilled the test of bravery that they themselves had already had to undergo – namely to jump off Herbert's hen-house roof.

So there I stood, teetering on the brink, petrified, with the mob gazing up at me and jeering that I was too scared to jump. They were absolutely right – I was too scared until Herbert pushed me and I had to. As far as I can remember, I was only a token member of the gang and so I didn't have to take any further part.

Winters in that little house were a test of endurance. There were no cavity walls or double-glazing and of course, no central heating. Fires heated the two living rooms but the bedroom didn't warrant a fire except in cases of illness. Then it was lovely to lie in bed and watch the flames dance on the ceiling. At least we had electricity!

It was while we were living there that I had my first taste of luxury. A fellow pupil at the dancing school had wealthy parents and when her sister was away, I was invited to stay in their (to me) palatial home. It is now an old folks' home.

A huge Lancaster would arrive outside our house – it overlapped next door as well – and Orchard, the liveried chauffeur, would come to the door to collect me and off I would go in state! Mr and Mrs Simms were kind and delightful people and it was there that I tasted asparagus and nectarines for the first time and played their grand piano.

Of course I always organised 'an entertainment' to be performed before leaving on Sunday evening. Once, at a children's party there we were all called on to 'do' something and so I duly obliged with a dance accompanied by Mrs Simms on the piano. At this point the Sheriff (and grandfather of the young hostess) arrived. 'You've just missed June's dance,' he was told and I was requested to repeat the performance. And so it became my proud boast that I once danced for the Sheriff of Nottingham.

One summer evening when my parents came to collect me my mother unwittingly caused me acute embarrassment. A large tennis party was in progress, everyone in their whites. I then spotted Mother arriving as if dressed for a society wedding. Poor love, she didn't get much opportunity to dress up but she'd chosen the wrong moment to do it!

They were such exciting visits to the Simms yet somehow they never made me feel dissatisfied with my own, far simpler life.

Chapter 3

Schooldays

I always had a keen ear for dialects and after a visit to London when I was very small, I startled my parents with a raucous 'Cor blimey!'

'Talkies' had arrived in the cinemas and soon I was speaking with a pronounced American accent. My parents sent me to elocution classes and that was how I came to meet my much-loved Ruth Derry. She taught voice production and persuaded me to sideline the American accent and speak good English but also other, local dialects. In so doing, she gave me a love of poetry, of Shakespeare and of acting.

Ruth saw me through all the London Guildhall grades up to, and including the LGSM diploma. This involved taking an oral and theoretical exam every year and the final examination entitled me to put LGSM (eloc) (elocution) after my name. When I was 15, she introduced me to the excellent amateur dramatic society of which she was the producer so that I could gain experience in playing before an audience.

By this time, we had moved once again to a bigger house on the outskirts of Nottingham and I was at the High School, a school I hated after the happy times at Mountford House, my first school. At Mountford House we sang French action songs as well as jolly English songs such as 'Hey-ho, Come to the Fair' and somehow we managed to learn a good deal, too. Indeed, when I was tested to determine which class I should enter at the High School, they found I was ahead of my age group.

In those days of discipline and academic goals my out-of-school activities of acting, music and dancing were frowned upon. I wasn't even allowed to do gym or play games because my health certificate stated that I had a congenital heart murmur. It was so slight that it had never held me back in any past activities – in fact I won the girls' sports prize in my last year at Mountford House. And then there had been Brownies . . .

Meetings were held after school and preceded by tea round the big dining table. My mouth still waters at the memory of the sticky buns – never since have I tasted buns with such a thick layer of lemon icing. Yummy!

Our pack twice took part in the annual concert of all the Nottingham packs of Brownies. The first year we did a singing version of *Cinderella* (me) and in the second year I was in a comedy role as the weather clerk in a tailcoat. I treasure the memory of another Brownie group, all portraying different flowers. One little girl, who had obviously been schooled to watch her aspirates, stepped forward and delivered her line: 'And hi ham the "Ollyock!"'

I was in the Pixie Six and wore a green badge. My bosom friend Helen was our Sixer and being two years older when she left it was I who replaced her.

At Mountford House we had a school library and I was able to take home a fresh book every Friday evening. Wherever I have lived since the first thing I do is join the library.

I did not want to go to the High School and it can't have been easy for my parents to pay the fees, buy the uniform plus all the books; it must have been galling for them to see me so ungrateful too. They only wanted to do their best for me and I don't know why I was initially so reluctant to go there. I soon began to realise that my resistance was partly justified, though.

After the happy songs of my prep school years I got off on the wrong foot with the singing teacher. He was a dour little man who began the lesson quite sensibly with breathing exercises, hands on ribcages and elbows out. I found that I didn't have quite enough room and so I turned very slightly sideways, but my action brought down the wrath of the little tin god.

'Why are you standing like that?'

'Because there wasn't room,' I meekly admitted.

'*Sir!* You call me Sir!' he demanded.

Not once did we learn a proper song. At the annual big night at the Nottingham Albert Hall for the school, staff and parents we sang our vocal masterpiece, 'Hannibal Crossed the Alps'. Mercifully, it was brief, consisting of about five bars. An imperious gesture brought us to our feet and an equally similar one sat us down again to cries of laughter from the audience. I can't say I was too surprised.

How different it was to my years of part-time study at the Stockwin Music College from the age of 12.

When I was in the lower school at the High School there was a marvellous teacher who dramatically brought to life the tales of the Roman Empire. Later, in the upper school, I have equally good memories of a teacher who conducted lessons entirely in French with the addition of animated mime. Those lessons were a pleasure rather than the chore of most of the others. I never learned anything in geography, for instance. To me, it seemed to entirely consist of lists of exports from countries, the situation of which I never found out.

Discipline was strict. We moved around the school in twos in a long crocodile, with not a word to be spoken. There was no speaking in class and permission had to be obtained before you could even open your desk. Maybe because I wasn't allowed to do gym or games I always felt slightly left out and this led to a spate of bullying from one hulking girl and her cronies. It consisted of a bit of pushing but I soon found a remedy: in a rough-and-tumble with a boy cousin I learned a useful tip and one day, on the way home from school, the occasion arose for me to put it into practice. I placed one hand on the girl's shoulder, the other behind her knee. After a gentle push she found herself sitting on the ground, grinning rather stupidly.

Later, I was invited to one of her parties and there I met her stepmother, to whom I took an instant dislike. The girl's attic bedroom was bleak and unattractive, so different from my own pretty room. Following this, I began to understand her a little more and felt some sympathy.

In spite of my love of stage appearances, off-stage I was a very shy child except with close friends. After a lesson on the construction of the sonnet when we were instructed to try our hands at writing one, though not as homework, I was apparently the only pupil to have done so. Being too shy to stand up in class and admit it, I quietly handed my piece to the mistress as she left the classroom. Though I waited in vain for her comments she never mentioned it. Here it is:

Childhood
The springtime of our lives, our childhood days,
When life's a game to play at with our toys,
The future lies concealed in a haze,
With all our future sorrows and our joys.
We spend the day in laughter or in tears,
As changeable as April is our mood,
At night, we know the same old baby fears
On which when we are older we shall brood.

And soon when we have fallen fast asleep
And everything is wrapped in silent gloom,
And as the moon ascends the heavens steep
It lingers, just to peep inside a room.
The moonlight shines upon a smiling face,
Ah me! She has not yet run in life's race.

I wonder, did the mistress perhaps think it too cynical for a child of 13 to have written? Certainly it was all my own work, perhaps influenced by the troubled state my mother was beginning to suffer from.

I was now taking yearly exams in music and elocution but becoming increasingly depressed at school. Asked to write an essay on the career that we would like to pursue, I wrote that I wanted to become an actress. The piece was returned to me ablaze with red exclamation marks (in those days, it was not an approved occupation). Of course nowadays any school accepts drama as a worthwhile subject for study.

Fortune telling and horoscopes are not for me. As Shakespeare penned in *Julius Caesar*:

The fault, dear Brutus, is not in our stars,
But in ourselves, that we are underlings.

But in Hamlet he wrote:

There are more things in Heaven and earth
Than are dreamt of in our philosophy

And I'm inclined to believe both sentiments.

How many times do you suddenly think of someone and a moment later the phone rings and it is that very person? It happens to me often. As a schoolgirl I had two rather weird experiences that I cannot explain. In my form at school was a girl called Marion. We were acquaintances rather than friends and we had no contact outside school. One night I had a vivid dream that she had died. It made such a terrible impression on me that I couldn't bring myself to tell anyone. For the rest of my stay in school I made a point of befriending her in class, but after I left I never saw her again.

Years later, on meeting up with another old classmate she said: 'Wasn't it sad about Marion?'

'Why?' I asked.

'She died – she was only 20,' came the reply.

I couldn't possibly have known what would happen unless some subconscious foresight had emerged in my dream.

Two or three years on a similar experience occurred. I knew two sisters and one night I dreamt that the elder one was killed in a car crash. A week later she was indeed involved in a road accident. She was unhurt but a woman in the other car was killed. I have had no such experiences since and if I've lost the power of foresight, apart from prior knowledge of phone calls, then I'm extremely glad.

On most days school lessons ended at one o'clock and I had to fit the daily prep in between music lessons on Tuesday and Thursday afternoons. There was a class in rhythm on Friday evenings and I spent the whole of Saturday morning in theory, choral singing and harmony. The grounding I received at the Stockwin Music College stood me in good stead when I had to sing during Children's Hour or play and sing on stage.

Some years later while working in rep I decided to have some more singing lessons and I was recommended to a teacher by a fellow actress. An elderly gentleman, he had an improbably full head of red hair. At first things went well but then he took to saying he wished I was his and chasing me round the room! Fortunately, he was a better singing teacher than a runner and so he never caught me. I decided he was too big a hazard and besides, it wasn't good for my breath control and so I left.

When I was not quite 15 my mother's health was deteriorating and she became convinced that she had a serious heart complaint and took to her bed. I raised no objections to leaving school to look after her and run the home while continuing my studies. Miss Philips, the austere headmistress, was much opposed to my leaving. When I went to say goodbye to her, along with all the other school leavers, all she could say was: 'Of course you know you can't expect to get anywhere without your School Certificate.'

Many years later I thought of her remark when I attended Buckingham Palace, where the Queen invested me with the OBE, 'for Services to the Performing Arts'.

Through my drama classes I had the chance to play Mustard Seed in *A Midsummer Night's Dream* at the Theatre Royal, Nottingham with Frank Benson's Company. I also donned a sarong and long black wig and brown body make-up to dance the hula-hula in *Aloma of the South Seas* with Emile Litller's Company, also at the Theatre Royal. In the same cast were Wilfred Babbage, John Salew and George Owen – actors I was to work with often in radio in the years to come.

A Nottingham matron was heard to remark that it was disgusting to have Burmese women in the show. My parents were not best pleased either at the state of the bath each night as I tried to wash off my body make-up!

A great event that took place each year was the Nottingham Goose Fair. It was – and still is – held at the beginning of October. When I was a child the Fair occupied the city square and most of the roads leading off it. Dragons, horses, roundabouts and a big swingboat with raucous music blaring away were all very exciting. Stalls selling sugar cocks on sticks and gingerbread and coconut shies filled the side streets.

After the square was landscaped and paved it became irreverently known as 'Slab Square' and the Goose Fair transferred to the Forest. Not a place of trees but a large open space, half a mile or so away from the city centre.

• Chapter 4 •

I Begin to Perform

After leaving school, sitting in my mother's darkened room for hours on end was hard for a teenager but she wanted me there in case she had an 'attack'. Once my father was home the evenings spent with Ruth Derry's amateur dramatic theatre group were my great escape.

My first appearance was as a schoolgirl and my schoolboy 'brother' was played by a spotty-faced little bank clerk, who gave me my first kiss backstage. Oh well, I thought, I had to start somewhere! Soon I graduated to juvenile leads and was given the opportunity to organise play-readings and direct one-act plays. I also picked up a few guineas modelling teenage clothes in fashion shows for two of the local stores.

When Mother's health improved a little I took a job as a junior governess at a small private school which enabled me to continue studies after school. Of the princely salary of £40 per annum I gave my mother £12 and somehow dressed myself by buying remnants in the sales to make my own clothes. The rest paid for my entertainment. A cup of tea and a toasted teacake before my drama lesson cost five pence (2p in today's coinage).

On holiday in Folkestone at the age of 16 I was given the chance to become a student with the Arthur Brough Players but my parents would not consider it. Though I longed to go to RADA, I knew they could not afford to send me there. I applied for an entry form and begged them to let me try for a scholarship – 'If I can't get in, I shall know I'm not good enough.' Again, they refused to contemplate it.

I had already entered (and won) a music festival and other competitions for verse-speaking when Father, reading from the local paper, announced: 'The BBC are having an exhibition in Nottingham and there's to be a talent competition. Why don't you enter the drama class?'

'Daddy, really!' I said, thinking talent competitions a bit beneath me.

'Cash prizes,' he continued.

'How do you enter?' I asked. Money was always in short supply.

And so I entered the competition with an excerpt from the trial scene of Shaw's *St Joan*. Wearing black tights, a short black tunic and a gold cross, I thought to myself, those who don't like Bernard Shaw may like black tights. Whatever it was I won and subsequently received another fee for appearing in the final night's show of all the winners. I needn't have been so snooty, either – the winner of the singing competition was Constance Shacklock, who later graced many a Last Night of the Proms singing 'Rule Britannia' and played the Mother Superior in *The Sound of Music* on the London stage.

I discovered that professional work could be had as an after-dinner entertainer. The problem was finding humorous monologues that weren't already too well known. 'Why don't you write your own?' suggested my father. He knew that often I had written funny poems for my own amusement and once started I discovered they flowed with hardly any effort.

Then there was an American series – they hadn't cured me completely! It was all about a dumb blonde in disastrous situations, a Cockney girl and a North-Country Cinderella. Soon I had a nice little connection going, all on recommendation. From that day on I've never needed an agent.

My audiences were all-male Masonic evenings. I waited in an anteroom until called and did two sessions of monologues. They were appreciative and ready to laugh – probably a good dinner and a drink put them in a receptive mood. I remember they once stripped the tables of daffodils and presented them to me, wrapped in a table napkin. A charming gesture.

Two books of my monologues were published. One by Samuel French which was used to train students at RADA, I learned years later. So even if I wasn't allowed to go there, at least my monologues did. I heard recently that a copy of 'June Spencer's Monologues' in Australia was offered on eBay for $30 – more than French's paid for it in the first place!

Odes and Oddities was published by Reynolds; also a one-act comedy. Both are long out of print though excerpts appear towards the end of this book. I also wrote a number of the 'Odd Odes' performed by the famous comedian Cyril Fletcher.

By the time I reached my late teens Father was lecturing on salesmanship at the Nottingham Technical College. When it came to the lecture on the importance of speech he would call me in to deliver it while he sat by (already I had attained my LGSM Performers Diploma).

Father also lectured at the Mansfield Technical College, some 14 miles away, and after making the usual contribution I was engaged for two terms on my own account. And that was how I found myself confronting a roomful of Nottinghamshire coal miners, all of them looking decidedly bolshie. It had been found that when it came to forwarding the men's careers, examiners in the oral interviews were unable to understand what the candidates were saying. In two short terms I was expected to make them intelligible. One of the more senior members of the class voiced their concerns: 'It's no good talking posh to them at pit bottom – you've got to swear at 'em!'

'Wouldn't it carry even more weight if you were to swear at them with resounding vowel sounds and smashing consonants?' I responded. At this, they all laughed and I'd won them over.

All I could hope to achieve in such a short time was to make them aware of the way they spoke and to make their speech more distinct. One evening I was very touched when one of them said: 'I was thinking about what you'd said about vowel sounds when I was at pit bottom the other day.' I hope I was able to help him – I'm very proud of those Nottinghamshire miners.

One of the young men was soon meeting me at the bus stop to carry my briefcase. I hope he survived the war and got the managerial role he wanted.

Shortly before the war my mother invested in a country retreat, which she had seen advertised in the local paper. But it was not so much country house as a disused single-decker bus, abandoned on a hillside near Newstead Abbey and very loosely converted to a place of habitation. Mounting the wooden steps, a corridor running the length of it housed a cupboard for food at one end, plus a large stone pipkin for water. This was filled by the bucketful from a pump at a smallholding at the bottom of the hill. Being 'delicate' Mother left that to the rest of us.

Inside was a small living room with a camp bed for my father, which doubled as a couch during the day. On arrival, we once discovered a mouse had made a nest in a cushion placed on the bed and we had disturbed her enormous family. They had also eaten a fair quantity of soap – I wonder what effect that might have had on them?

The remainder of the bus was divided into two bedrooms: the first for my mother and through that my little room could be accessed. We once managed to entertain one of my boyfriends on leave from the Navy. He had my room, while I shared with Mother. The fact that Fred had to go through our room to get to his caused a certain amount of hilarity and inconvenience.

Talking of convenience, there was an Elsan closet in the little shed outside; also a larger shed used by the men in which to wash and shave, provided they remembered to take a bucket of water with them. The 'grounds' consisted of a large plot, where I grew spinach and clove carnations, which I sold to a local greengrocer. The spinach was much in demand.

We had a paraffin lamp for when it grew dark in the living room and candles for the bedrooms. There were stables nearby and I would often hire a mount and hack through the country lanes on my own, bareheaded, without a thought for safety.

Mother paid £80 for the property and I think it was money well spent. Often at weekends the car would be loaded with food and bedding, plus our wire-haired fox terrier Nick. Mother and Father would drive there while I followed on my bicycle. At last I had acquired one and I cycled miles on it.

In fact, we were staying there when Nottingham experienced its worst air raid: we could hear the crumps of the bombs and the sky was red with the fires. We worried about what we might find on our return but the bombs fell several miles from where we lived.

We had some happy times on that funny old bus, living the simple life. I think they kept it until I moved to London. I suppose it was the forerunner to my house in Menorca, but that comes much later on in this story. Sadly we lost our little dog Nick when we were there. One day he disappeared and wandered as far at the main road, where he was run over. He was a thoroughbred and highly-strung which could make him slightly unreliable, although he was very attached to my father. Mother kept well away from him, but he managed to nip a few people and once caused the vicar to take flight when he came to call, scattering pens from his pocket and other possessions en route.

Nick wasn't averse to being dressed in a large doll's dress and coat and dancing down the room on his hind legs. Indeed, he was the star turn at one of my parties.

In 1939 I auditioned for the BBC. I arrived at the Birmingham Studio expecting to audition for revue with my monologues only to discover it was a drama audition. No problem! From memory, I re-enacted scenes from several plays, taking all the parts. I then did the revue audition.

I don't believe auditions have changed very much over the years.

I was alone in the studio, the producer auditioning me was in the control room. He could talk to me through a loudspeaker, telling me what he wanted me to do. If one is being auditioned for a specific role another actor will play the other character in dialogue.

I was thanked formally and went home, receiving a letter a few days later to say I had passed the audition. My elation was short-lived. War was shortly declared and Midland Region entertainment programmes closed.

• Chapter 5 •

The War,
Marriage and Rep

When I was born, just after the First World War, fashions hadn't moved on much from Edwardian times. In the earliest photos of my mother and me her dresses were almost ankle-length, her long hair piled high. She was very proud of her beautiful hair and used to say that it was 'long enough to sit on'. Although short hair became fashionable in the twenties, Mother wasn't 'bobbed' until well into the thirties.

Queen Mary kept her Edwardian image until she died early during the reign of our present Queen. In those days the privacy of the Royal Family was absolute and respected. The goings-on of the younger members were not reported in the press and glossed over to such an extent that the general public knew nothing of the Prince of Wales' enjoyment of other men's wives. Until the abdication crisis not a clue did we have of his affair with Mrs Simpson: along with most of the female population my mother was besotted with the handsome young prince so it must have been a big letdown when the news finally broke. George VI, that rather remote but respected monarch, uttered his final words, which were reported to be 'Bugger Bognor', and died, leaving a new king who refused to ascend to the throne without his twice-divorced lover.

It just wouldn't do, so the shy but well-liked George took on the heavy mantle of the throne with the greatly loved and radiant Elizabeth supporting him. The Coronation was celebrated across the country and I was invited to an all-day party of young people. We were to start with tennis but it rained and so we went to the cinema instead. In the evening the dinner dance was somewhat spoilt for me by my then boyfriend having too much to drink and dancing all night with another girl. Never mind, I spent the evening with a far nicer chap!

The Royal Family refused to remove to a place of safety when the Second World War broke out and faced the danger of bombing with everyone else. Buckingham Palace was hit, Princess Elizabeth joined the ATS and Margaret fell in love with her father's equerry. If only she had been allowed to marry him, how different her life would have been. Soon after, with Edward forced to abdicate through marrying a divorcee, poor Margaret was persuaded that it would not be right to marry a divorced man when she was second in line to the throne.

Public opinion has since moved on and although there was at first opposition to our own Prince of Wales divorcing and then marrying a divorcee, the Duchess of Cornwall has won our approval through the unassuming way in which she supports the Prince and the warmth of her personality. His first marriage, however, had all the pomp and ceremony of a Royal wedding.

My mother and I were on holiday in Eastbourne when the Germans began bombing Poland on 1 September 1939. That evening we sat on the blacked-out promenade listening to the band playing all the popular songs of the First World War. My mother joined in the singing with enthusiasm, which surprised me as she had lost her favourite brother in that war. I was silent, thinking of all the boys I knew who would be joining the forces.

Father drove down to take us home as the trains were full of little evacuees, their names and destinations on labels tied to them, carrying gasmasks. They were such sad, bewildered-little figures heading for strange places, not knowing when they would see their parents again. On the way we stopped and bought blackout material. The next day we listened to the tired old voice of the Prime Minister Neville Chamberlain on the wireless telling us that we were at war with Germany. The year before, when he came home with his 'piece of paper' promising peace in our time, no one had really believed it.

The night before that I, together with many of my young friends, was at a Full Dress ball. Some of the boys had already joined the Territorials and were in Mess Dress; it made me think of another ball on the night before Waterloo. The boys went out to buy the late-night papers telling us that war was at least postponed. Now it had come.

Nothing much happened for several months and we called it the phoney war, and then the Germans were on the march. The ships set sail to rescue our troops at Dunkirk and Winston Churchill put heart into us with his fighting speeches. His words have echoed down the years for me and when things have gone wrong in my life, I'm able to say, 'Never give up.'

I shall never forget the day when the Germans marched into Paris because it was 14 June and my twenty-first birthday. I had made a beautiful white lace dress: it had puff sleeves and a sweetheart neck and I wore a spray of my favourite pink roses. My parents had booked a hall that was in a beautiful rose garden – the perfect setting for a summer party. There were 42 of my friends there, including all my boyfriends, and so I danced with each of them in turn. I knew it was probably the last time we should all be together as they would soon be joining the forces.

Such a beautiful day, it seemed wrong to be having a big party but it had long been planned and so we decided to go ahead with it. One by one they went, including a fair-haired blue-eyed boy with a cheeky grin called Roger Brocksom, whom I had met on holiday in Chapel-St-Leonards when we were both 17. There were two cafes there and each ran informal dances patronised by groups of teenagers, mostly from Nottingham. Two of the groups merged and we danced together. Roger always delighted in telling everyone in later life that he had 'picked me up at a sixpenny hop'.

I remember telling him loftily that I would be his girlfriend for the duration of the holiday, but after that we would finish. I couldn't bear holiday romances that petered out during the winter! Yet somehow he always seemed to be around. Although his home was in Grimsby, where his father was a schoolmaster, he soon came to Nottingham University before going into the Army. His persistence finally paid off when he came on leave and proposed, though it wasn't exactly romantic. He said: 'How would you feel about being married to a Second Lieutenant?' I replied: 'I wouldn't mind if it was you.' It was some weeks before we were officially engaged because he had to save up for the ring. Eventually he said: 'I could spend £10 and not miss it.' So I knew it wasn't going to be the Koh-i-Nor. Actually I beat him up to £12.

Roger was serving in Northern Ireland and our banns were read in Armagh Cathedral. He came over to go on a motorbike course, had an accident and hurt his leg, then ended up in a military hospital in Lincoln that had once been a mental asylum. I visited him there and it was then that he told me he'd saved enough for the ring and we could get officially engaged. Naturally, being Roger, he told everyone that he'd officially proposed while in a lunatic asylum.

When I told my father that Roger had saved enough for a ring all he said was, 'Well, he doesn't want to run himself short.' It was all very prosaic.

Our wedding was on 27 May 1942. The big local store had one wedding dress in my size. It cost £7.7s and seven coupons – by then, clothes rationing had come in. Assuming from the banns that I was marrying an Irishman, the organist entertained waiting guests with a selection of Irish airs. We were married by Bishop Neville Talbot who was 6ft 7in tall plus mitre and he greeted me from a great height on the chancel step with: 'Cheer up, June!' I had never been so nervous in my life and it showed.

As we drove away from the church Roger said: 'You've done it now – you've got yourself a name nobody can spell!' He was quite right: my favourite mis-spelling of my married name was 'Mrs Buxom'.

Roger had only a week's leave and one day had already been used assembling for the big day so we had six days in Matlock, where we played a lot of table tennis.

Being wartime we hadn't been allowed to have icing on the cake. It was covered with white rice paper instead. I had a much better wedding cake when as Peggy I married Jack Woolley! At least my father had been able to get a case of decent champagne. We saved one bottle all through the war and opened it to celebrate Roger's homecoming.

Nine months after the wedding Roger was posted to India and then Burma, where he was in charge of building forward airstrips in the jungle. It was hard to have to part, but it was just the same for so many other young couples at that time and I simply went on living with my parents. It was three years and four months before we saw each other again. By then he was a Major and my life had completely changed.

Until my marriage, I had done a war job in the Nottingham City Treasurers Office and continued with my after-dinner entertaining, and then one day a friend of Mother's who had a connection with the Little Theatre in Nottingham rang me to say: 'They're looking for a child actress to play Miranda in *Quiet Wedding*. Get down there and tell them you can do it!' I went to the stage door and met the producer, who told me flatly that I was too old to play Miranda but I was overjoyed to be offered another role.

This was twice-nightly weekly rep and by Friday I had learnt my role but they still didn't have their Miranda. A member of the cast who had seen me play child parts (I was small and very slim) said: 'Give it to June – she can do it.' So, at that late stage I switched characters. After the first performance it was very gratifying to have the producer come round to the dressing room and say: 'I apologise for saying you were too old to play Miranda.'

The following day when I arrived at the theatre I was greeted with 'Where were you this morning?' Apparently I had become a fully-fledged member of the company for the princely sum of three guineas a week. At that time the Equity minimum was £3. I was handed a book with a very large part to play the following week. Somehow I still managed to cope with the few private pupils that I had also taken on at home, both elocution and piano. One of them did brilliantly in her exams.

It was a bit difficult while I was at the theatre. Mother didn't get up until late so I had certain chores to do at home first. Whenever she heard me using the carpet sweeper she would call down: 'That needs emptying!' Funny how such things still raise a smile after 60-odd years.

Rehearsal was at 10 so I had to leave home at 9.30. We rehearsed until 1pm then it was home for lunch, perhaps a piano lesson and then back to the theatre for the first performance at 4.15pm. On the days when I didn't have a pupil I often stayed on after rehearsals for a snack in the Milk Bar – where are they now, I wonder – and then on to a free pass at the cinema. We rarely saw the end of the big feature but if we didn't appear in the play until Act II then we stayed a little longer and would have a bit of a rush to make it on stage in time – how blasé can you get?

I sometimes wonder how I managed to learn a new role every

week with such a full schedule. As the 'juvenile' the size of my lines varied from week to week. Some weeks would give me nice fat roles and at other times I could be the maid with few lines. It was a wonderful experience and should be part of every actor's learning curve. Sadly, though, these days there are very few of the old weekly reps left, where actors can get their grounding. Often it means that an actor goes from television or films to their first work on stage only to be completely inaudible.

My father once said to me: 'I sat at the back of the balcony this afternoon. I could hear your every word.' My reply was: 'I should jolly well hope so!' I was trained to project my voice and I can still do it. At my ninetieth birthday party, which took place in a large hall, I raised a laugh. After some lovely tributes from various people I began my reply with 'I don't need a micro-phone.' Afterwards the director Graham Gauld said: 'And I could hear every word!' Echoes of my father . . .

That year at the theatre I played everything from juvenile leads to an old woman, a Chinese houseboy, a 40-ish tart – and of course, every child part that came along. To quote one press critic on my performance as Button in Ian Hay's *The Housemaster*: 'There were two outstanding performances. One is that of June Spencer as the irrepressible 'Button'. Seldom indeed is the sight of adults taking juvenile parts entertaining: this is one of the exceptions'.

Act I ends with Button appearing as one of the schoolboys in shorts, blazer and school cap. My parents came to see the show and didn't recognise me – they thought I was one of the schoolboys!

When I first joined the company as Miranda in *Quiet Wedding* it seems the handsome young juvenile fell rather heavily for me. Later he was heard to remark rather dolefully, 'I thought she looked about 16, and I hoped she was 18, but then I found she was 23 and married!'

But I mustn't forget the theatre cat. Usually it was content to hang around the dressing rooms, delighting to sit on my shoulder and play with the long blonde wig I wore as Fan in *The Light of Heart*. One night it obviously felt it should play a more visual part in the production and made its entrance through the fireplace onto the stage in the midst of a rather dramatic scene, to the delight of the audience and the consternation of the actors. That was the end of its acting career and it was thereafter banned from the theatre.

Nottingham had only one serious raid but we had frequent air-raid sirens as enemy planes passed over en route to their targets. In our air raid shelter in the garden we had two bunk beds for Mother and me: my long-suffering father had a sleeping bag on the floor. We wore 'siren suits' like those worn by Winston Churchill but ours were brighter colours. For the whole of one winter we slept in there and never had a cold. As soon as we moved back into the house we all caught colds!

I would sit in the shelter reading Roger's frequent letters. He wasn't able to tell me much but it was comforting to know that he remained safe and was still in India. When he landed in Bombay, as it was then, he was able to meet up with my uncle and his family. Uncle Cecil, my father's youngest brother, had been in charge of the Bombay Tramways Company: upon the outbreak of war he was made a Major and continued to do his old job.

As I sat in my primitive little shelter I would read Roger's descriptions of going racing in Poona and the mouth-watering meals he had enjoyed. Later, when he went into Burma, things were very different for him: driving through the jungle, clearing space and building forward airstrips so that the fighting forces were kept supplied by plane. By then letters to him were mostly written in my dressing room at the theatre, telling him about all the plays we were doing.

As the war went on food rationing became more stringent and clothes rationing also made life difficult. One had only so many coupons which had to be surrendered when anything was bought and sometimes it was hard to choose between buying a pair of shoes or a skirt. I had to provide my 'wardrobe' for the roles I played in the theatre except for costume plays, the clothes for which were hired by the theatre. Luckily I had a good stock of dresses (mostly homemade) when the war started and I was lucky in that Mother and I were the same size – she often saw her own dresses on stage! I once cut up a pretty voile nightdress to make a dress for one of my child parts.

We saved our stockings for when we played leading roles but otherwise we would put make-up on our legs and draw a 'seam' down the back with a make-up stick. Tights didn't appear until much later, silk stockings were unobtainable and we had to make do with artificial silk. Nylons were a luxury still to come. It was also very hard to buy theatrical make-up. Fortunately I knew the owner of the theatrical costumiers in Nottingham.

We were twice nightly. The first performance was at 4.15pm and the evening one started at 6.30pm. This was because the buses stopped running at 9pm, so we had to be pretty smart in getting off our make-up if we needed to catch a bus to get home.

Things were all very amicable until the Christmas show became imminent. It was to be a three-week run of *Alice in Wonderland* and I would play Alice. At three guineas for 12 performances, it worked out at 63 pence a performance – just over 25 pence in today's money – so I asked for a rise. The manager said he couldn't pay any more. Besides, hadn't he just had me deferred from being called up again for war work? To me that smacked of blackmail so I drew myself up to my full 63½ inches and said, rather dramatically: 'I had rather fill shells than work for you, Mr Wright! You'll have my notice on Friday.' With that, I marched down to the Labour Exchange and told them I would be free for war work.

And so I became a 'Hello Girl'. Nowadays we can dial anywhere in the world. In those days a trunk operator was needed at a switchboard to route a call, sometimes through three or more other operators, and in the run-up to D-Day the lines were frantically busy with Army personnel trying to drum up supplies. After my shift finished I was off with a Voluntary Entertainment company for the forces. We had a repertoire of two plays and away we would go in a cranky old bus with our scenery stashed down the centre aisle, for all the world like a fit-up company.

We never knew what to expect until we got there. It might be a draughty Nissan hut converted to a theatre or an aeroplane hanger but it was always perishing cold and I wore a sweater under my evening dress. We were never sure what the stage would be like until we arrived either and often we had to reverse our scenery because there was no way onto the stage from our usual entrance.

On one occasion at a convalescent home the 'stage' was about 8 × 5ft. Until then they had only a singer or instrumentalist to entertain them. We solved the problem by ignoring the stage and performing on the floor, using the door to the room as our entrance – the French windows were just where they should be!

In one of our plays, J.B. Priestley's *Dangerous Corner*, we had to take up our positions on stage during a brief blackout. My night vision is not good and I would make for my chair in the dark and never sat down until I could feel both arms. On one memorable occasion I felt both arms and immediately sat down on the floor! I'd had a hand each on the arms of two chairs and sat down between them. Up in a flash, I was properly seated when the lights went up but the rest of the cast were puzzled as to why I appeared to be trying hard not to 'corpse' (laugh) for the rest of the play.

We always received a warm reception from the troops and were well entertained in the Mess afterwards. RAF stations were our favourites because they would give us a good meal of bacon and eggs – such food was in short supply for civilians.

But I hadn't let my professional career lapse for once again I applied for an audition at the BBC's Midland Region, which in 1943 was starting up again. Edward Livesey, a brilliant and prolific features writer and producer, put me through a rigorous audition and two days later I swapped shifts with another girl and went to Birmingham for my first broadcast, in which I played a child – and that was when I sounded the fire alarm!

Ted Livesey told me later that he had not been at all pleased to be interrupted in his work to come and listen to my audition but he added that it was the best one he had ever heard. Whatever, I owe him a tremendous debt for giving me my chance in radio. His much too early death was a tragic loss.

This was the first of many child parts because I soon became a stalwart of Children's Hour. With elderly Dorothy English and Jill Nyasa playing convincing little boys, we three 'children' totalled about 130 years between us. Not long after that first broadcast I had the chance to let Roger hear my voice. The Midland Region was doing a programme called *Home Town*, in which the wives of soldiers overseas could record a message to their husbands. Roger was in India and so in the hope he could find a radio to hear my message, I sent him a rather cryptic cable just giving him the time and radio station. Extremely puzzled, he found a fellow officer with a radio at whose home he was able to listen. Needless to say, he was thrilled to bits to hear me talking to him.

Chapter 6

The World of Radio and *The Archers*

With the arrival of VE Day I was able to give up my job at the telephone exchange and concentrate on broadcasting. I couldn't throw myself whole-heartedly into VE celebrations because Roger was still in Burma and the war with Japan not yet over. Although I loved the theatre, I knew that when the war was finally won and Roger came home I should not want to leave him and follow a stage career. He was an engineer and would have a nine-to-five job, so radio was my best option.

By now I had moved to London where most of my work was, though I still travelled frequently to the Birmingham Studios in Broad Street. Roger would soon be returning and I wanted to make a home for him to come back to. I found a very large room on the first floor with a view over Kensington Gardens; the bathroom was two floors up and shared with about five other people. Any water I wanted was transported from there in a large jug then carried back up again as slops but to me it was paradise.

It was the London home of the then Lord Aberdeen, a charming old gentleman who had sold the lease but retained the floor above me as his London pied-à-terre. The new owners were a delightful Irish couple and her brogue became the source of the voice of Rita Flynn – but that is jumping the gun . . .

It was there that I acquired my beloved cat, Candy. I had begun to be visited by a mouse which skittered around my room and for some reason reminded me of the then Prime Minister, Clement Attlee. I called it Clem. On mentioning this to my landlady – who was horrified – I said that what she needed was a cat (I love cats). She said, 'If you'd like to have a cat that'd be quite all right,' – this in spite of the fact that my rent book said no cats, dogs or pigeons. I consulted the cards in the local paper shop window and there, sure enough, was one seeking homes for a litter of kittens. A fellow actress in a nearby house gave me Candy in exchange for a bunch of flowers.

Then came the long-awaited day when Roger would at last be home. Late one night at the end of May 1946 I went to the station to meet him. A group of travel-weary officers disembarked from the train and we met and kissed for the first time in three years and four months.

I had laid the table for a meal to welcome him with our silver and glassware wedding presents but he was too tired to eat anything. At first he was not welcomed by Candy – she bitterly resented having to share me with him! However, she moved house twice with us and was a beloved member of the family for 16 years. For another year Roger remained in the Army, stationed in Devizes, and between broadcasts I would go down and stay with him at a nearby hotel. It was there that we struck up a friendship with an American Army officer and his wife.

One day she asked if I would mind if she did her piano practice on the piano in the lounge. Of course I said it was fine, expecting scales and studies. Imagine my amusement when with one finger she proceeded to pick out a popular tune of the day: 'Mairzy Doats and Dozy Doats'.

With Roger's demob, the next thing was for him to find work as a civilian. He had gone into the Army before completing his degree but at 26 he didn't feel like going back to finish it. Finally he got a job in the London office of Palmers Hepburn but had to do six months' training in Newcastle in the steel construction division of Vickers Armstrong. We were separated again! Occasionally he came home for the weekend and I visited him in Newcastle.

By the time he came home again we realised it was time to move to bigger premises and said goodbye to the theatres, Kensington Gardens and being on the doorstep of Broadcasting House – but it meant that I would have a garden again. So Roger, Candy and I moved to our first house in Worcester Park, Surrey. It had two reception rooms, a minute kitchen and three bedrooms plus a big garden with plum and pear trees.

What a wonderful time it was to be in radio! Television was not yet a rival, the stars of radio were like those on TV today and we were much in demand for opening fêtes and bazaars. In the summer, we rarely seemed to have a free weekend. After *The Archers* started, fêtes and personal appearances took me all over the country. I was once flown to Cornwall in an old Dakota aircraft. It was not so long after the war and the plane was quite a primitive adaptation to passenger use. We appeared to be transporting a miniature zoo in the cabin with us, including a parrot whose squawks seemed to imitate every rise and fall. Roger, who knew Dakotas, said: 'You won't fly over the hills, you'll go round them.'

I was opening the proceedings at a mass meeting of the Women's Institute and such was the popularity of *The Archers* that I was mobbed, much to the consternation of the organisers, one of whom shouted: 'Keep back! Do you want to kill her?' It was quite a scary situation.

Listeners have their own mental images of how a character looks. On meeting me, most people say, 'You look just how I thought you would,' but at one fête I was accosted by a little old lady who studied me from head to toe then pronounced judgement: 'You're not very big,' she observed. 'I'm bigger than you,' was my answer. And so I was.

In those days radio programmes were 'live' and when the green light came on in the studio you knew millions were hearing you – no 'fluffing' your lines! Children's Hour was always a joy to do. Peggy Bacon produced it in the Midlands, with a prolific output of plays and serials for which we returned each week at the same time for every episode. I played Mary, Queen of Scots and Florence Nightingale as well as innumerable child characters.

It was at this time that I began working with Norman Painting – Phil in *The Archers*. We appeared together along with Denis Folwell, later to be Jack Archer, in a series called *Through the Garden Gate*, a fantasy play with music. I played a little girl called Judy, Norman was a character called Froo, Denis was Bogey-Bo and Bob Arnold appeared as Old Crusty the gardener, later to be Tom Forrest in *The Archers*. The script was by Edward J. Mason, who with Geoffrey Webb went on to write *Dick Barton* and later still *The Archers*.

As well as Children's Hour, work in classic drama serials, plays in verse and features kept me busy in London and other regions. With the encouragement of Edward Livesey, I began to write again too. He produced three of my satirical feature scripts: *Man the Hunter*, *The Vanities of Man* and *The Rivalries of Man* – which gave lots of work to my actor friends! They all received good press notices when they were produced as well.

Graham Gauld now took over Children's Hour and I particularly remember the 'Simple Simon' programmes every month. The irrepressible comedian Leonard Henry played Simon and I loved working with someone who made me laugh on the radio as I was growing up. There were always songs to be sung and the writer was Norman Painting, who also composed some of the music.

Each Christmas we did a 'Simple Simon' radio pantomime before a studio audience of children – I remember one in which the cast was like a preview of *The Archers*. The Dame was Philip-Garston-Jones (the first Jack Woolley), hero and villain 'doubled' by Arnold Peters (the present Jack Woolley) and I, of course, played the Princess.

I was now working with the legendary voices of radio. Gladys Young always dressed elegantly and never removed her beautiful hats as she worked in the studio. That very beautiful actress Anne Cullen remembers being taken quietly to one side by Gladys to be told: 'We don't wear trousers to the studio, dear.' You should see what is worn nowadays – anything goes! Then we believed in looking smart at all times.

Many was the time I worked with Marjorie Westbury (tiny and rotund but sounding like the most glamorous heroine such as Steve in *Paul Temple*), James Mackechne (leading man in so many plays), the incomparable Carlton Hobbs, Wilfred Babbage from the *Aloma of the South Seas'* days, Philip Cunningham, Philip Wade and Norman Shelley, who infuriatingly insisted on smoking a cigar at the microphone and filling the studio with smoke. There's no smoking anywhere in the BBC now and a good thing, too. Then there was Bryan Powley – known to us all as 'Uncle Brian' – who never wrote his name on his script, just 'Not yours'.

One of the best-loved producers among actors was R.D. Smith. Reggie was a big man with a big heart and many was the time he would give an actor down on his luck a break. I was in his very first production for BBC radio, a 15-minute play called *The Luddite Lovers*, with Marjorie Westbury as my mother. It was then that Marjorie taught me how to cry on radio. Reggie rehearsed us hard for a solid two days – I don't think he ever rehearsed much again!

Part of the cast would have a 'read through' and the rest would appear later, then all would adjourn to the pub for 'lunch', where one or two other out-of-work actors would be added to the company, with some of us told to 'give them a few of your lines'. Afterwards, we would return to the studio for a run-through for timing. We had been doing a weekly series called *First-Hearing* – live, of course. On one particular occasion Reggie found the script was much too long and minutes before transmission gave us massive cuts, removing whole pages from the script. As the red light began to blink, showing that we were almost on, the programme assistant rather anxiously said: 'Reggie, you do know we have 40 minutes today, not 35?' So, we all had to scramble to reassemble our scripts.

It was not unknown for Reggie to tiptoe into the studio during transmission. Leaning over your shoulder while you were at the microphone, he would cut several of the lines you were about to speak with a pencil. Somehow we got through!

On one occasion a rather scruffy-looking young man wandered over to me in the studio and seemed rather anxious about the poem he was to read in the programme. I thought he looked like one of Reggie's 'down-and-outs' so I made encouraging noises to him. A few days later I saw his photo in a magazine: it was Dylan Thomas.

When Reggie retired from the BBC he took a Chair at Guildford University. The last time I saw him I was returning from a recording in Birmingham. As I ascended the escalator at Waterloo station I could see Reggie descending on the adjacent escalator. When we passed each other we smiled and I said, 'Just come from Birmingham,' and he told me, 'Just come from Guildford.' Those mundane words were our final farewell after so many years of working together.

I arrived early at the studio one day and already an exceedingly pretty girl, who shyly asked if I could explain a point in her contract, was there. After that we worked together many times.

She was so earnest about her career and one day she confided, 'I've been offered the BBC rep, but I'm not getting any stage experience – and I'm nearly *16*!' I treasure the memory of her running up and down the studio, shouting in a cockney voice, 'Don't forget your pure ice cream!' It was one of a series of feature programmes on London, this time about the street markets and inspired by Dr Johnson's observation that, 'When a man is tired of London, he is tired of life.'

I felt that if there was any justice in the world she would go far. And so she did. Shortly afterwards she was chosen by Charlie Chaplin to be his leading lady in *Limelight*. Her name, of course, was Claire Bloom. Someone once said they thought Claire was my younger sister – I was flattered! I have always followed her career with great interest.

During the war Wilfred Pickles had created a stir as the first newsreader with a North Country accent. However, I knew him as an actor and worked with him many times. I played opposite him in several serials adapted from the novels of Arnold Bennett. Graham Gauld, who had now moved to London where he came to be one of the BBC's most prestigious drama directors, directed these. Wilfred and his wife Mabel, a lovely, homely couple, were inseparable. They once very kindly gave me a lift home from a party. Their car was a two-seater and I travelled on Mabel's knee – no seat belts in those days!

For many years Programmes for Schools gave me regular work and I cannot remember the number of times that I sang the milkmaid's song in the programme about Jenner. We rehearsed from 10am and went live on air at 2.20pm or thereabouts. Many times, I was given several verses of a song and asked to 'make up a little tune'. As each verse naturally had to have the same tune, I would spend the coffee break drawing a staff on the back of my script and composing something suitable.

In a 20-minute programme we all had many parts but some

lovely roles came my way and I especially enjoyed playing Lady Jane Grey and Lorna Doone.

While I was still living in Nottingham and commuting to the Birmingham Studios it meant changing trains at Derby. On a very rare occasion I left the studio feeling depressed. What was wrong I can't remember but I do know that as I crossed the bridge at Derby I felt like giving up altogether. As I went down the steps to the platform I saw my train leaving. It was the last straw and I was almost in tears. As the guard's van slowly went past, the guard called out: 'Where to, luv?'

'Nottingham,' I replied.

He stopped the train and said: 'Jump in, luv!'

As I settled down into my seat I thought to myself, he was kind to me so I won't give up. That guard will never know how he may have changed my life.

Derby station figured in another incident. After the war, but while Roger was still in the Army, we arranged to meet at my parents' home in Nottingham for Christmas. It was the day before Christmas Eve and I was doing a live broadcast in Birmingham called *Music at Christmas*, in which I was playing the Virgin Mary. How, I wondered, do you portray Mary through voice alone? Calm and tranquillity, I thought.

After the rather late transmission and feeling I might be sickening for a chill or even worse, flu, I caught the train to Derby. My connection was waiting so I got in and off we went. Although I was expecting a fast train to Nottingham, we set off at a decidedly leisurely pace. I remarked on this to my fellow passengers: 'We shall be late getting to Nottingham at this rate.' To my horror they informed me that it wasn't going to Nottingham and the first stop would be Uttoxeter. There had been two trains, back to back, and I'd got in the wrong one.

When I disembarked at Uttoxeter a lone porter was closing the station for the night. Again, I was shown such kindness. He carried my bag to the nearest, rather primitive hotel, where I phoned Roger.

'I shan't be home till tomorrow,' I told him.

'Why not?'

'Because I'm in Uttoxeter and there aren't any trains till morning.'

'What are you doing in Uttoxeter?'

'Don't ask!'

I found a bathroom, but with no light bulb. Despite this I had a hot bath in the dark and felt much better in the morning.

In later years, when commuting from Surrey to Birmingham, I had some horrendous train journeys at weekends when most rail works take place. My cross-country journey involved at best two trains but on one occasion there were three trains and three buses – it took practically all Sunday. That sort of caper became too much for an old lady and nowadays I get special dispensation of a lift in a car.

To revert back to the feeling of depression on leaving the studio, I can think of only one programme that made me feel I hated my job. I was not alone – almost the whole cast, including Jill Balcon who was playing the lead, felt the same.

It was a production of Lorca's *Blood Wedding* and was being directed by a very temperamental guest director more accustomed to operas. We suffered five days of absolute hell. He didn't know what he wanted, only what he didn't want, and none of us could do anything right. When he finally got it in the can, he burst into tears. Not the sort of behaviour we expect at the BBC.

Although the war was over by then there were still many restrictions and heating was one of them. During the bitter winter of 1946/7, I was in a weekly programme called *The Table on the Terrace*. It was a classical music programme with a live orchestra linked by three characters and a waiter – played by Dino Galvani of ITMA fame.

We began rehearsals in a large studio in Piccadilly wearing our overcoats, but the brass instruments were playing flat because of the extreme cold. So we all had to up stumps and move to the Maida Vale Studios, which were warmer. Unfortunately, the invited audience could not be contacted in time and so they missed the show.

Now I come to a show that everyone remembers: *Dick Barton, Special Agent* burst onto the air to the tune of 'Devil's Ride'. Dick, Snowy and Jock, played by Noel Johnson, John Mann and Alex McCrindle, was a 'must' for millions of listeners at 6.45pm. In several stories I was the girl who was either tied to a chair in the cellar with the water rising, or locked in a cupboard to be rescued at the last minute by the dashing trio.

Gunshots were frequent and filled the studio with smoke, or if the gun failed to fire (as it sometimes did) a good gunshot effect could be obtained by striking a screen with a stick – and without the smoke! During a simulated fight it was quite a sight to see several grown men running round the microphone, hitting themselves on the shoulder and shouting: 'Ooh!', 'Ah!', 'Take that!', 'Agh!' and 'Ow!'.

The programme originated in the Birmingham Studios then moved to London, where we recorded in the studio in Tottenham Court Road. At that time there were recording studios all over London.

Once *The Archers* was well established, it was decided to drop *Dick Barton* and put the series on in its place at the time-slot of 6.45pm. Dick, Snowy and Jock have been active ever since in films and recently a spoof stage version – yet another memorial to Ted Mason and Geoffrey Webb. Long may they continue!

Mrs Dale's Diary, another daily serial, was also running at that time and when I worked with them, I came in for a bit of teasing for being 'the spy from the other camp'. The powers that be once decided to hold a joint *Archers* and *Mrs Dale's Diary* party for publicity purposes. It was a disaster! Gwen Berryman (Doris in

The Archers) informed them she had never listened to their programme. They wanted to announce that our Polly Perks was secretly engaged to a young actor in *Mrs Dale's Diary* until she put her foot down in denial, while Jessie Mathews spent the evening complaining to me that it wasn't her fault that she had replaced Ellis Powell and the listeners were blaming her for Ellis's death. It wasn't a jolly evening.

In those days many classic serials were broadcast from Bush House for the Overseas Service and they provided me with many wonderful roles. So now I have arrived back at the instant when someone said to me: 'You're going to be in *The Archers*, aren't you?' It is customary to be approached by the BBC and offered a role so it was odd and a bit annoying to learn of an engagement in this way. It appears that Godfrey Baseley, full of enthusiasm for his new idea, had been telling all and sundry about the proposed casting.

The story of how *The Archers* came to be has been told so often: how, at a farmers' dinner, one of them said: 'What we need is a farming *Dick Barton*' and Godfrey had the foresight to take it on board. The *Dick Barton* writers, Ted Mason and Geoffrey Webb, were commissioned to produce a pilot of five scripts and a nucleus of seven actors assembled. Norman Painting and I were two of that seven. We were told: 'This is not a drama production – the characters are to be real-life people overheard.'

We recorded the episodes on giant discs as was the custom at that time and these were transmitted during Whit Week of May 1950. Afterwards we heard no more until December of that year, when we learned that the pilot episodes had been well received. We were offered a three-month contract to record six episodes a week over three days to begin transmission on 1 January 1951.

The fees offered reminded me of my theatre rep experience. I was on the top rate of £12 for the six episodes, others were on £10 and even £8 but there was plenty of time to do other work.

Peggy's 'pregnancy' of the spring episodes came to fruition soon after the programme started and Anthony William Daniel was born. Mrs P (Pauline Seville) arrived to supervise the birth. Pauline was a smart, pretty woman who, she told me, had always played character roles from the moment she left drama school. Although playing my formidable mother, she was actually several years younger than me.

For photo calls she would don unfashionable clothes, hideous hats and a glowering expression. Her outraged 'Mister Gabriel!' to Walter, who determinedly courted her but to no avail, was one of the delights of the early years. She was greatly missed after her much-too-soon illness and death. Sometimes I hear echoes of her in Peggy. I like to think she is becoming more like her mother as she ages. She has all the strong-mindedness and a sense of what is right and what is within the bounds of propriety.

Gwen Berryman (Doris) carried on the Gladys Young tradition of wearing pretty hats in the studio and she and Harry Oaks (the first of four Dans) were given the chance to exercise their good singing voices in family singsongs with Phil at the piano. Although a spinster, Gwen fell comfortably into the role of the motherly Doris. She loved the children of members of the cast and treated them as generously as if they were her own grandchildren. In the end, I think Gwen began to believe she really was Doris Archer, though she did admit to being afraid of cows! She had a special chair in the Green Room because of her arthritis – which she said started when she was chased by a rhinoceros on safari in Africa.

When she was young Gwen had been engaged to a doctor, who died tragically. She was a professional singer and stage actress before she came to us, always in awe of the editors of the programme especially as she grew older and more frail; I still remember her delighted chuckles when something amused her.

The pace of the programme was leisurely with specially composed music linking the scenes, but the now-familiar signature tune, 'Barwick Green', was by Arthur Wood. We early members of the cast were given the chance to listen to several pieces of music as possibilities. I wasn't keen on Godfrey's choice of 'Barwick Green' – I thought it sounded like a march – but now it's hard to imagine anything else.

For our first photo call we went to the farm on which Brookfield was modelled. There, we met two farmer brothers. One of them addressed all and sundry as 'Me old Pal, me old Beauty,' so Walter Gabriel was not so much a fictional character as a mirror held up to nature!

For a long time while we were a very small cast we were called upon to double many other characters. My main double was Rita Flynn. Arnold Ridley, later to be the loveable old Private Godfrey in *Dad's Army*, played Doughy. Arnold was the author of *The Ghost Train* that has to be one of the most frequently produced stage plays ever, barring Shakespeare! He once told me ruefully that he had sold the copyright early on and so he must have lost a fortune in royalties.

Bob Arnold – a fine singer of folk songs and a genial personality, a true countryman – soon joined us as Tom Forrest and his old country songs were often heard.

Meanwhile, the feckless Jack Archer, played by Denis Folwell, was already causing Peggy heartache. Sometimes he also made things difficult for me. Denis liked his drop of scotch and he would rather unwisely spend the lunch break in The Crown. There were times when I had to hang about until he was able to play his scenes with me to the satisfaction of Tony Shryane, our director. When Denis was on form we worked very well together, though.

One has to be very careful about having a drink at lunchtime when working. I learned my lesson early on in my radio career. I was working in a somewhat technical feature programme and had just one full page of rather uninteresting content to read. Also in the programme was one of the radio greats, Mary

O'Farrel. She kindly took me out to lunch – with wine. We were live on air that afternoon and I got through my long speech without any problems but it might have turned out otherwise! I have never drunk since if I am working in the afternoons.

Of course, the axe falling on *Dick Barton* brought protests from the many fans. One of those who bitterly resented it was a young Terry Wogan. Nevertheless, I think he has forgiven us for he asks *The Archers* to lend their support with his Children In Need Appeals. He once joined us to take part in a specially written episode and is just as charming and natural as you would expect.

Godfrey Baseley directed the first few episodes of *The Archers* and then handed over to Tony Shryane, who steered us through the first 25 years until his retirement. We all had great affection for him.

Chapter 7

Old Friends and Red Letter Days

In addition to directing *The Archers*, Tony Shryane devised and produced *My Word* and *My Music*, highly successful programmes that ran for years, and also another of his successes, *Guilty Party*, in which I frequently appeared.

This was an ingenious format, starting with a short murder play and then the actors, in character and off-the-cuff, were grilled by a panel consisting of John Arlott, Fabian of the Yard (the real one) and F.R. Buckley. The 'guilty party' could lie but everyone else had to tell the truth. As this part was unscripted, we had to be very much on our toes to get the facts right.

As much more was recorded than would be used often we said outrageous things to try and 'corpse' the panel, knowing this would be edited out. One fateful day, however, I was listening to the transmission at home and to my horror there was no playlet but it went straight into what was soon apparent as the unedited version of the cross-questioning. What risqué things had we said? It was quite some time before someone realised and substituted a piece of music instead – aptly titled 'It Might As Well Be Spring!'

Later, we did a television version and as it was 'live', this was quite a test of nerves and we had to discipline ourselves when it came to the 'grilling'.

On one occasion I shared a dressing room with Courtney Hope, an elderly actress who looked like a dowager duchess. Before transmission that day, she paced up and down, saying, 'Please God, let it be alright; oh God, let it be alright!' Her prayers were answered – and it was. She was a devout Christian, who delighted in having the young curate to tea and entertaining him with risqué stories. I could well believe it.

After rehearsal one day when she was unable to get a taxi I persuaded her to take the Underground with me. As we sailed down the escalator she said in a loud voice: 'When I'm on these things I'm always convinced I'm going to fall flat on my arse!' A few steps down from us a young man turned round, saw the elegant, elderly lady and from the look of disbelief on his face was saying to himself: 'No, I must have misheard.'

Before that my only TV appearance was in a factual programme from Alexandra Palace in the early days. Live, of course, no zoom to camera – it came right up into your face. To see one's face in it, upside down, was very off-putting. I was never keen on doing TV and didn't do another programme after *Guilty Party* until I was in my eighties.

One day I was phoned and asked if I would be interested in doing an episode of *Doctors*. I told them thank you for asking me but I don't do anything involving learning lines any more. 'That's alright,' they said, 'The character has had a stroke and can't speak.' Well, that was different! I accepted the part and had a wonderful time.

At one point in the action Christopher Timothy had to drag my unconscious body out of a gas-filled room and then give me the kiss of life. I thought, this is rather nice – I'm enjoying this but then the real ambulance crew arrived and said: 'No, he wouldn't do that – he'd put her in the recovery position and wait for the ambulance.' Rotten spoilsports, I thought.

A taxi driver I've used regularly in the past in Birmingham said, 'I saw you in *Doctors*. I hardly recognised you with the old make-up.' I didn't tell him that I wasn't wearing any! TV cameras are not kind to old faces.

In the last 10 years I have lost both my husband and my son. That has taken its toll, so when I needed a new passport I looked at the photograph in the last one showing a rather pert blonde and realised I couldn't get by with it again. So, for the first time I ventured into one of those minute kiosks to get a new photograph. Heaven knows I'm not very big but with my handbag, shopping bag and umbrella I was pretty firmly wedged. Next, I needed my glasses to read the instructions and six pounds' worth of small change. It swallowed my only two-pound piece, never to be seen again. I ended up feeding it with five-pence pieces which fell out of the slot and there was no way I could pick them up.

Why don't they tell you the seat is adjustable? The machine wouldn't accept my crouching in front of the stool and my final position of raising my bottom a few inches off the stool by propping myself up with my arms inevitably resulted in a portrait of a very pained-looking woman. A neighbour signed that it was a true likeness, though recommended I don't show it to anybody. But I digress . . .

One of the most famous moments in *The Archers* was the death of Grace on the night when commercial television began. The series scooped the headlines then and we did it again on the fiftieth anniversary of commercial TV. This time it was Peggy's vanquishing of the awful 'Hazel' and the question of the paternity of Emma's baby. We stole all the publicity!

Poor 'Jill'! – she still lives under the shadow of Grace. Grace is dead but she won't lie down. Patricia Greene, Paddy to us all, followed Gwen Berryman into Brookfield as Jill, the perfect farmer's wife to Norman Painting's Phil. And now it's the third generation with David and Ruth.

One of the secrets of our success is the way the programme has kept up with life as it has changed over 60 years. Not only in farming matters, which are accurately reflected as they are today, but in the fact that all the characters have aged. Those of us who were young when the programme first started are now grandparents and in Peggy's case, a great grandmother.

In 1967 it was decided to tackle the problem of illegitimacy – a very daring storyline for the times. So, Jennifer Archer became pregnant but it was some time before it was belatedly realised that somewhere there had to be a father and we had heard nothing about a particular boyfriend. It had to have been a clandestine association with someone, but who could it be? Finally, it turned out to be Paddy Redmond, a farm worker.

In the meantime, as Jennifer's mother I received some letters whose writers were getting mixed up between fact and fiction. One listener wrote:

Dear Mrs Archer,
    Just a few lines, did you know that your daughter Jennifer is expecting a baby in six months' time? I always listen to the Archers affair everyday.
    Yours,
    Archer Fan
P.S. There's only three people who know about it. The Doctor, the Vicar and your daughter Lilian!

I didn't need to reply – there was no address. Another came from two sisters:

We sincerely sympathise with you for the terrible heart-breaking news you will receive from your daughter Jennifer sooner or later; but you poor dear you have <u>really</u> guessed! as instinctively a Mother would; dear Peggy we are <u>very</u> sympathetic to you! a great Sorrow! maybe will lay you low! your parents the Archers will rally round you and Jack your husband you will find hidden depths of love and kindness in him, as to Jennifer! I do not know what his <u>hidden</u> depth of character will do about her!! He may punish her beat her or lock her up in her room and she will have to accept it!! No good in brazenly not being ashamed! (If one is <u>not</u> ashamed of <u>that</u>!), there is nothing else worth being ashamed of! . . . Find the father and <u>make</u> him marry her, is the only way to peace and happiness again in the Archer family. deep sympathy to you all'.

Another missive put it more succinctly:

I think you ought to know that your daughter Jennifer is going to have a baby. Only three people know. The vicar, the doctor and your daughter Lilan.

Why don't you know? Don't you listen to the programme?

Adam, the baby in question, had a rather traumatic childhood. He lived with Jennifer at The Bull until she married Roger Travers-Macy. There was great consternation when Adam was kidnapped as a little boy of three and held to ransom. Luckily the police found and returned him unharmed. His troubles weren't over, though. The poor little chap was bitten by an adder and nearly died. Perhaps it was no wonder he went abroad as soon as he was old enough and only came home many years later! Peggy was glad – he had always been her favourite grandson.

I have a special memory of one listener. When my young son was a pupil at the Rambert School of Ballet he was a bit of a prankster and so one open day when I was told that Dame Marie

Rambert herself wanted to speak to me I was a bit apprehensive, wondering what mischief he had got into. All the legendary lady wanted to say to me was: 'I know you can't tell me, but shall we eventually know who is the father of Jennifer's baby?' Dame Marie was a keen fan, it transpired, and listened to the Omnibus every Sunday.

On another occasion, I accompanied a friend to a recording of *Any Questions?*, to be held in a local hall. As we went in, I submitted a question, as requested, and as luck would have it, mine was one of those chosen. I gave my married name and asked the question. Several days later I received a letter from a listener via the BBC. It said:

Dear Peggy Archer. What were you doing on Any Questions? You're not REAL, are you?

The mind boggles! We appeal to such a wide range of listeners: the farmers, the lonely, blind listeners, eminent professors and surgeons . . . I was once informed that as I lay unconscious on the operating table the topic of conversation was . . . *The Archers*.

By 1954 we had moved to a much bigger house and garden in Walton-on-Thames. Once we were settled in, Roger joined the Round Table – the under-40s part of Rotary, and I joined the wives in the Ladies Circle so we immediately had the friendship of about 20 couples of our own age. Once a month we met for dinner and all had a project of service in the community.

We had some very enjoyable social events as well, with an annual supper dance – on one occasion with a cabaret performed by the 'ladies'. I recall a spirited can-can and I produced and danced in the Charleston number.

We once held a party for all the members' children at our house. Each brought a present, which was to be sent to a children's home. To my horror I found a very small David behind the Christmas tree quietly opening them all! Then, one summer, we had a barbecue and barn dance in the garden with lanterns hanging in the trees, which looked enchanting. There were many happy times there, as well as some sad ones.

I have two special memories of David and my father there. The first, when a strong, upright man walked round the garden, his arm on the shoulder of his little grandson, both in earnest conversation. The other, many years later, when a tall, strong young man walked with his arm round a bent, frail old man, still in deep discussion. There was tremendous affection and respect between them.

The Archers has given me many enjoyable experiences. Cruising the Baltic with several other members of the cast and entertaining our fellow passengers was great fun.

In 1973, the year we joined the Common Market, such was the popularity of *The Archers* on the Continent (they could listen courtesy of the Forces Network), that it was decided the cast should pay a visit to Holland. We left the studios at Pebble Mill in a single-decker bus emblazoned with a large banner on the side, saying 'Ambridge to Amsterdam' and drove to Hull, where we embarked for the overnight crossing.

Gwen Berryman, who by then was rather frail, spent the night in the sick bay as the many steps down to the cabins defeated her.

I shared a cabin with Gwenda Wilson, 'Aunt Laura'. This was below the waterline with rather primitive washing facilities. Gwenda and I retired early. Not so the two actors in the next cabin. We were rudely awakened by shouts of rather tipsy laughter and learned the reason the next day. One of them had brought a brand new pair of pyjamas and omitted to take the pins out before attempting to put them on.

Once ashore, we drove many miles to Schiphol Airport to pick up the members of the press who were to accompany us and had elected to travel the easy way and fly. Already we had recorded scenes with the captain on the way over on the boat and the next day we were to record further scenes at a radio station. It seems there were two radio stations and we went to the wrong one, but we got it right at the second attempt! After that we became tourists and thoroughly enjoyed our visit.

As the fortieth anniversary of the programme approached it began to be hinted to Arnold and me that the big story would have something to do with Jack Woolley and Peggy Archer. There was to be a celebratory Ambridge rose cultivated by the famous David Austin and it would be the gift of Jack to Peggy. For this recording we went to the Chelsea Flower Show on press day. We arrived there in the morning and the exhibiters were still preparing their stands. To us, it seemed impossible that it would all be ready in time for the Queen's afternoon visit.

Arnold and I were photographed with David Austin and the rose – 'Jean Paul' – in attendance, and we recorded the scenes that would later be heard in the programme. After lunch we were free to wander round and view all the beautiful displays. It was such a privilege to be able to see it all without the usual crowds – we just had to be out before the Queen's party arrived!

Both of us were given several bushes of 'our' rose. Arnold's flourished – and mine faded away over time. Although in the past I had won prizes with my roses at local amateur horticultural shows somehow I or my roses have lost the knack!

That was our fortieth year and the culmination was the wedding of Jack and Peggy. For many years Jack Woolley and Peggy's relationship was solely on a business footing, with Peggy owning and running The Bull while Jack had Grey Gables. When Peggy gave up the pub and went on to manage Grey Gables, Jack began to take a more personal interest to the extent of proposing marriage, much to her embarrassment and she turned him down. After all, her experience of marriage to Jack Archer wasn't particularly happy, especially in the last years before his death. So, Peggy distanced herself from Jack and seemed content to be a lone widow. However, Jack was never one to give up easily and eventually she became fond of him, especially after his accident when he fell off the roof – which medical opinion considered may have triggered the Alzheimer's in later years.

So, this time when Jack proposed, Peggy accepted and she came to love him deeply. But as soon as marriage was mentioned Jennifer was up in arms. She did not relish having the Brummy-accented Jack as a stepfather until Lilian came hotfooting it from Guernsey and forcefully pointed out that their family wasn't exactly out of the top drawer. As she put it: 'We've pulled ourselves up by our boot-straps.' So, Jennifer capitulated and the wedding preparations went ahead.

But this wedding was not only going to be heard – it would be seen as well. I was let loose in one of the big London stores to choose the dress and was anxious that it should be something suitable for an elderly bride. The one that was found for me was ideal: it was in ivory georgette with a high neck, long, full sleeves and a long skirt. I decided it needed a small hat in coral. That was more difficult to find, but we eventually ran one down at a trade show in Birmingham. As soon as I saw it, I said: 'That's the one!' It was fine straw and had a little veil. Later it was sold on eBay.

A Birmingham store provided me with a pretty skirt and made a little blue velvet jacket for the going-away outfit. Very generously, they allowed me to keep it. The lovely blue hat was from the same store as the wedding gown. Because it completed the outfit so well, I decided to buy it – at the full price!

Arnold Peters, the elusive Higgs and I spent a day on a photo-shoot at Ambridge's 'church' and 'Grey Gables', together with the Bentley and Captain, the dog. We started first thing in the morning at the church in our wedding outfits. No one else there. Then we moved to the 'reception' venue and were photographed with the wedding cake and in the Bentley. We then changed into our going-away clothes for a session. Because for some reason another photographer couldn't be there while the BBC one was shooting, we had to start all over again for the new one. We changed clothes so many times that day that we all felt quite frazzled by the end of it!

I had a beautiful Christmassy bouquet and there was a wonderful two-tier wedding cake decorated with the Ambridge roses in sugar. I still have one of them!

The actual 'wedding', of course, was on 1 January and we were photographed and filmed for television standing in a group on the steps of All Saints, Langham Place. Hoards of photographers were grouped in the road and at one point everything ground to a halt when an old lady pushing her shopping trolley came between us.

She stopped and gazed round her. 'What is it?' she asked.

Someone said: 'It's *The Archers* – Jack and Peggy's wedding!'

'Oh,' she said, 'I never watch it!' and walked on. I for one certainly saw the funny side of it.

We all adjourned to Broadcasting House where the 'reception' was to be held. At my suggestion the wedding party lined up to receive the guests as at a real one and in they came – crowds of VIP guests. There were the usual speeches, notably Jack May as best man. The cake was cut and champagne flowed freely – the BBC did us proud that day. No recession in those days!

That evening we had a big party at which our husbands and wives could join in and I remember saying to Arnold's wife Beryl: 'You can have him back now!' It had all been so 'real' I almost began to feel as if I'd married Arnold, but Roger was there to prove otherwise.

Shortly afterwards, on Valentine's Day, Arnold and I were invited to appear on *Pebble Mill at One*. We both had the same idea – a Valentine card was slipped under my dressing-room door which said: 'I love you Mrs Woolley' and I returned the compliment, but mine to Arnold simply stated: 'Roses are red, violets are blue, I committed bigamy marrying you' – just another case of mixing fact and fiction.

We were invited to appear in a big charity variety performance at the Alexandra Theatre in Birmingham in the presence of Princess Anne – so I was presented to her for the second time on 28 April 1991. The cast of *Me and My Gal* were down from London and our contribution was to join in 'The Lambeth Walk'. Earlier in the day we rehearsed in the theatre bar. We were planted near the back of the stalls and at a given point members of the chorus descended into the auditorium, grabbed the guest 'celebrities' by the hand and raced us up onto the stage, where we sang and danced 'The Lambeth Walk'. It took me back to pre-war days when the show first appeared and we all did 'The Lambeth Walk' at dances.

The entire cast and us joined in the grand finale, singing, 'There's No Business Like Show Business' – which proved half of us didn't know the words and we were reduced to faking it!

It was later that same year 1991 when Roger rushed into our room before I was really awake. Full of excitement, he handed me a letter from the Prime Minister's Office. It had been sent to ask if I was willing to accept an OBE. *Would I?* I just couldn't believe it – and Roger had known for months that my name had been put forward, but hadn't breathed a word. He had been consulted by phone for details about me from the BBC.

We hired a chauffeur-driven car for the great day. Owing to the many bomb scares at that time all cars had to park opposite the Palace to be examined by the police. Once given a clean bill, we proceeded across the way. It was the thrill of a lifetime to be able to drive into the forecourt of Buckingham Palace.

Roger and our daughter Ros had to go in by one entrance, I by another. Later, Ros told me she was so impressed by the model guardsmen lining the corridors that she prodded one with her finger and was mortified to discover he was real!

I made my way up a sweeping staircase and into the Picture Gallery, where we were all briefed and arranged in the correct order before marching off to the ballroom. The Queen stood on a low dais, guarded by Ghurkhas, and as each name was announced we went forward, one by one.

I had been practising as I wanted to do a deep curtsey and I managed it without mishap. The band was playing all the time but I was too excited to notice what the music was. Her Majesty is clearly given a quiet word to identify each recipient for she knew I was in *The Archers* and said it was listened to all over the country. The investitures are now videoed so I have my own personal, visual record of our conversation. Afterwards we were entertained to lunch at the home of Graham Gauld, who wanted to hear all about it.

When we got home I was tired but happy. I changed out of my smart suit and put on a tracksuit. Then I pinned my OBE to my chest and had a nice cup of tea – the end to a perfect day!

Another lovely memory was of being in Horse Guards Parade for the Queen Mother's 100th Birthday Pageant. Arnold and I, together with our producer, scriptwriter, sound engineer and a runner, were seated among the audience to record Jack and Peggy's reactions to it all. Part of it was scripted, but part was 'off the cuff' and as soon as it was complete, the runner – a young member of a Birmingham Athletic Club – took the tape and ran with it from Horse Guards to Broadcasting House, where it was cut into the same evening's episode. A runner was quicker than the risk of the tape being snarled up in London's traffic.

Afterwards, we sat back and enjoyed the wonderful spectacle. My most treasured memory is of the Chelsea Pensioners marching proudly past and that amazing 100-year-old lady standing for them as they passed her. Thousands of rose petals showered down and I still have some of them – a fragrant and treasured memory.

Chapter 8

My Island Paradise

In 1972 Roger and I took an Easter break in Menorca. We hired a car and explored the island, arriving towards the end of the holiday at a headland from where we looked across the inlet to a cluster of houses round a small beach, backed by three palm trees. It was a cold, drizzly day but we decided to drive round to have a closer look.

At the edge of the village was a sign 'Para Vender' and we walked round on the rocks next to the sea to see what was 'for sale'. The end house, half-built, was without the means of getting upstairs so we went into the ground floor, where I gazed out of the hole in the wall destined to be a window. I saw small islands and a distant lighthouse. At that moment I knew with absolute certainty that this was where I belonged.

I said: 'Magic casements opening on the foam of perilous seas in fairy lands forlorn' (Keats' 'Ode to a Nightingale'). Casa Ruisenor, the house of the nightingale, has been my beloved bolthole ever since. For 37 years it has been a place of laughter and friends, and sometimes a few tears. It was not long before I met Bob and Josie Pitcairn who lived nearby, which was the start of what has been a valued and enduring friendship. The same can be said of Francisco, my friend and general factotum.

Peggy and I have our differences, but we both love our gardens and share a love of cats. Sammy, Peggy's legendary cat, must have been the oldest one on record but she was finally laid to rest and she now dotes on Bill and Ben, the two new cats.

The feral cats in Menorca have been such a big and rewarding part of my life that it would be impossible to write this story without giving them their rightful place in it. Because I am away from home so much, I cannot have a cat in England but over the years, Roger and I have befriended and have had the affection – not entirely cupboard love, we hope – of upwards of 15 cats. The most we have ever had at any one time was nine.

Roger would say, 'There's more washing up for the cats than for us.' Each time we arrived they seemed to know we were coming and they were waiting for us – and most of them managed to get through the front door before we did. Roger was never happier than when sitting on the terrace, binoculars to hand and a cat curled up on his knee.

Shandy was a sweet-natured cat, a little street-wise mother who was forever washing her almost full-grown kitten Smoky, me, my husband . . . anything that moved and breathed was washed with loving care. Soon I was besotted enough to allow her to sleep on my bed and I would wake in the night to find her on my shoulder, paws round my neck and my face being given a thorough going-over with her rough tongue.

If I had occasion to visit the bathroom in the night she would accompany me and for her part would hop into the bath and position her rear end directly over the plughole, afterwards trying to tidy up by scraping the side of the bath. I explained that a flush from the tap was all that was necessary. The first time she did this I was amazed at her ingenuity and instinct of cleanliness that led her to seek out and use the outlet of a bath when she had probably never seen one before.

In appearance she was mostly tortoiseshell and had the pointed face and large ears of many of the Menorcan cats, showing her probable descent from Egyptian forebears. Menorca was invaded by so many races over the centuries due in great part to the port of Mahon being the largest natural harbour in the Mediterranean and so descendants of ships' cats may have also contributed to the wide variety of breeds among the feral cat population. Without the benefit of watching TV commercials Shandy knew the trick of inserting a paw into anything she couldn't reach with her tongue and I once caught her on-camera with her paw in the milk jug. At least she had the good grace to wait until I had finished with my breakfast tray!

It was fascinating to watch how she prepared her young one to survive in the harsh environment into which she had been born. After washing her, Shandy would then attack her fiercely and at first we were horrified to see these noisy and apparently vicious fights until we realised that Smoky was being trained to defend herself. The spat over, they would share a chair for a long siesta together.

Eventually there came a time when we arrived to find that although Smoky was still there, Shandy had not been seen for some time. Someone said she was pregnant again and although I toured the village with her photograph, no one had seen her and I was never able to find any trace of her. I still miss her.

Smoky was not a case of like mother, like daughter. As well as an almost total dissimilarity in appearance, she was very much her own cat. Her dark grey and white coat was thick and looked almost more like wool than fur. She was beautiful and she knew it. Like any star she loved to be photographed and went to great lengths to give me interesting shots – for example, lying on a plate of apple peelings, including the knife, or posing by a vase of flowers in the hope of appearing on a birthday card, perhaps?

Certainly she was a bit of an exhibitionist. If she suddenly disappeared in a closed room we looked ceiling-wards. There she would be, gazing down on us from the top of a range of cupboards, or picking her way daintily through a display of china ornaments and we knew that with her they were safe.

Smoky loved to go for walks with us, sometimes running ahead, sometimes dawdling behind and stopping when we did to talk to friends. She would also go to the beach with us and wait patiently while we played boules and then accompany us home again. When we played Scrabble she took an interest, but when she'd had enough she walked over the board without disturbing a single tile.

As our 'family' of cats grew she registered her disapproval by refusing to have anything to do with them, growling fiercely as she escaped past them. Finally, she took herself off and we didn't see her all summer. However, as soon as her new adopted family closed their house for the winter, Smoky was back. To our pleasure we found that she had lost much of her former aggressiveness. In the past when it was necessary to move her from her favourite chair it was advisable to wear a stout pair of gloves for she would growl like a dog and follow that with a sharp nip.

Gentle, self-effacing Cleo – black as the night, with beautiful eyes – appeared in time to produce two kittens in the bushes on the cliff-side near the house. They were in a safe nest but we could watch the young family through binoculars from the terrace. As soon as they were grown enough, she arrived on the terrace with the little black one in tow. 'This one,' she seemed to be saying, 'Is yours.'

My husband always said that at that moment Pickles, as we soon named him, decided he was a human being and took over the house and us. With his tiny, pointed face, huge ears and eyes that looked like two lamps in a coalhole, he was obviously of Egyptian ancestry. He was completely tame and loved to be picked up and petted. Unlike most cats he would stay where he was put and any stranger was a mate of his.

Visiting friends would be met by Pickles at the end of the road and escorted home, him bringing them proudly up the steps. A familiar voice on the terrace would draw him from his favourite chair in the house to welcome the visitor. Because everyone doted on him we knew he would survive comfortably when we were not there although we once heard that he very nearly didn't make it. It seems he fell, or was thrown from the cliff into the sea by some boys and he was seen to strike out and swim until rescued by a young holidaymaker. One of his nine lives was gone!

He expended another by developing a large tumour in his ear. Our wonderful vets operated and to everyone's relief, he came safely through. After he refused point-blank to wear the Perspex collar to prevent him from scratching until the stitches were removed, we had to keep him under observation day and night for two weeks. He slept on my bed and whenever he stirred, I woke.

When our friends invited us to go to them for drinks, we said: 'Sorry, we can't leave Pickles.' To which they replied, 'Well, bring him with you.' And so we did. He accepted a harness and lead without demur and blithely trotted off with us to a couple of parties, where he was spoilt rotten but behaved impeccably. It was soon discovered that he loved olives, especially those stuffed with anchovies. Thereafter no uncovered dish of olives was safe from him. He would steal one and play with it, patting it round the room and finally devouring it with great relish. Pickles also behaved impeccably when the vet removed the 12 stitches from his ear without any need to anaesthetise him. We were so proud!

Like Smoky he too enjoyed a game of Scrabble, perching on Roger's shoulder and advising him what to do, or sitting on my knee and watching every move. Sometimes he couldn't resist joining in, and wondering where my seventh tile had got to, I would eventually find he was holding it in his paw! Unlike Smoky, however, when he decided that he had had enough, the tiles were scattered left and right as he walked across the board and that was the end of the game.

Pickles' trust in people unfortunately extended to cars. He simply didn't seem to realise they spelled danger and many was the time when he would be sitting in the middle of the road as we drove up and we would have to stop, get out and take him in the car while we drove into the garage. One sad day a vehicle coming too fast into the village was the death of him. He was only two and a half years old, but he had given so much affection and pleasure to so many people. He was, indeed, a very special cat.

Pickles' tabby brother was beautiful but as nervous as his sibling was tame. Terrified of everything and everybody, he would venture up on to the terrace but on being approached, he would rush madly away, but always towards the imagined point of danger. If footsteps were heard coming up the steps then he would immediately hurtle down them, nearly tripping up the visitor. When someone emerged from the house he would dash into the house and then out again.

Whenever I put a dish of food down for the cats he would spin round three times, knock it over and having frightened himself half to death, would rush away and miss his dinner. That, you will readily understand, is why we nicknamed him 'Panic Button'. In time he ventured into the house just far enough to share a chair with Pickles . . . so long as no one came too near.

We were only able to stroke him once: we found him one day – a big, beautiful, healthy-looking cat, lying on his side and panting. So we carried him gently to the car to rush him to the vet, but sadly he died before we had driven a mile.

Of Cleo's first lot of sextuplets only the two tabbies survived.

Like flowers, two little faces would gaze through my window when I opened the shutters each morning. The tamer of the two was so sweet we called her Honey-bun and we were delighted when she was offered a proper home in a nearby town. The other flower-face we named Flora, but in the fullness of time it became obvious that no self-respecting tomcat would be able to face his mates with a name like that, so we hastily changed it to Flurry.

He was one of the more nervous of the cats, which placed him in good stead when the vet arrived to neuter them. Flurry immediately went to earth under the far corner of my bed and didn't reappear until long after the vet had gone!

Cleo's final set of sextuplets consisted of two tabbies, two black and whites and two strange-looking scraps of dark tortoiseshell with such weirdly marked faces that they looked like a couple of small witch doctors, hence Hoodoo and Voodoo. Hoodoo didn't survive for very long, but Voodoo – a bossy female – is still very much with us and has more to say for herself than all the others put together. She is almost unique in this. Most of the others only utter loudly when food appears. Otherwise Smoky growled, Pickles emitted minute squeaks and Cleo only ever meowed to call her kittens to the milk bar.

The only other survivor of that last litter is a handsome black-and-white cat. At first he was known as Smudge but as his personality and character developed, he eventually earned the name of Charlie – after Charlie Chaplin. This was partly because of his little black 'moustache' and partly because he's a born loser.

Charlie was always very timid with the other cats and when food was put down, he was the one who was crowded out. If you think of musical chairs, invariably Charlie was the one who was 'out'. Of course I take pity on him and he knows I shall catch his eye and put down a separate dish out of sight of the others. Perhaps he is not such a 'Charlie' after all!

Eventually we reached the conclusion that the time had come

to put an end to Cleo's production line of kittens and she was duly 'done'. For 13 years she lived a life of ease, with her remaining offspring around her, still snuggling up to their mum. With her usual gentle good-humour, she tolerated them and she and her boyfriend – Long Tom, as black as herself – would companionably share a cardboard box together. Sadly they both died on the same day. Long Tom was found dead outside the house and Cleo in a neighbours' garden. We never knew the cause of the tragedy.

A few days before the sad demise of Pickles there appeared on the terrace two cats that no one had ever seen before in the village: a handsome tabby, clearly in charge, and a beautiful little pale grey and cream cat with aquamarine eyes. We could only think they had been dumped from a car and from our observation of them since we could almost hear the tom saying to his little sister: 'Don't worry, I'll look after you – I'll find us somewhere.' His devotion to her was charming to see.

We called them Misty and Minder. Both were very tame – they had obviously been house cats and one wonders how anyone could have been so heartless as to turn them adrift. The moment I settled on my sun-lounge they were up there with me but if I picked Misty up, Minder became anxious and a worried paw would pat my foot until I put her down again. Should there be a spat among the other cats, he would check at once to make sure she was not involved. We have noticed similar solicitude before between a tomcat and a kitten of a later litter. Pickles and Honey-Bun were inseparable until she was adopted.

Some months after the arrival of Misty and Minder it became obvious that Flurry found Misty irresistibly attractive and it was also apparent she was not averse to his attentions. We feared that although she was so tiny and very young, we thought, she would be due to kitten about a week before our next visit. I left a comfortable box for her on the terrace and friends agreed to visit and feed her every day.

When we arrived the box was empty but Misty looked much thinner. The next morning when we awoke the box contained three tiny kittens. She had carried them home in the night from where they had been born. We were so touched that she had brought them to us. The two tabbies' eyes were open but the little black tom's eyes were still closed. We thought that Cleo's friend, black Big Tom, must have also paid court!

The three kittens, enchanting as they were, took a terrible toll on Misty. Their insatiable thirst reduced her to skin and bone in spite of the extra nutritious food we gave her. We would see her toiling up the steps, a plump kitten hanging askew from her mouth, bumping it on each step because she was too small to lift it high enough. She was a good, if harassed mother and it was a relief to us – and I'm sure to her – when the kittens were found a home, all three together, on a nearby farm. When she had recovered her strength we took her to be spayed and now she is once again plump, with a beautiful thick coat.

The cats obviously find other people to feed them when I am not there for they always look sleek and well fed when I arrive. Misty, Voodoo and Charlie are now the only ones left. I hate leaving them and they seem to know when I am going. On one such occasion Charlie came in with a live, but stunned fledgling sparrow and laid it at my feet, looking up at me as if to say, 'This is to thank you for feeding me.' I said: 'Oh Charlie, I really wish you hadn't!' and carried it to a nearby garden in the hope that its mother would find it.

A few minutes later Misty appeared, carrying a dead fledgling sparrow (the same one, I wondered). She too laid it at my feet as if to say: 'You liked Charlie's present so I've brought you one, too.' What can you do?

One is tempted to think that because Menorca is in the Mediterranean it must be hot and sunny all the time. Islands tend to be breezy and that is very welcome in high summer when it can indeed be extremely hot, but strong winds can also whip up the sea: the sun shining on really rough waters is a glorious sight.

Every so often it is brought home to me how very powerful the sea is. My house is built on rocks overlooking the sea and once it was more or less *in* the sea! On one occasion, a week after I left, we had a tsunami. I was told that the level of the sea rose considerably and eventually a huge wave swept along the village coastline. Breezeblocks were tossed eight feet onto a terrace, the wave smashing down my very heavy wooden garage doors. It pushed my car into the wall of a shower room, dislodging tiles inside, and then swirled into a downstairs guestroom, bringing debris and soaking everything in its path.

The wave moved on, smashing down a garden wall and flooding houses along the quayside. Boats were sunk, one never to be seen again. How thankful I was that I wasn't there when it happened.

Roger and I spent several Christmases in our Menorcan home and had lovely weather but every few years it can snow, occasionally quite heavily. These days the weather seems topsy-turvy everywhere but I think of Menorca mostly when it is calm and peaceful, the sea a deep blue, waves lapping on the rocks below. There cannot be a more beautiful view anywhere in the world than the one from my terrace – that's what I think, anyway!

Because of the large yacht marina in the next inlet there is a constant flow of luxury yachts and cabin cruisers sailing by. Roger used to like to sit on the terrace, monitoring their progress. Sometimes a crew appeared not to have consulted the charts beforehand and so they would not heed the buoys, take the wrong course and go aground on a sand bar or worse, on the submerged rocks. One such cabin cruiser became wrecked on rocks offshore in full view of the house. It stayed there for months, slowly breaking up, until one stormy day when it finally went under. I saw it go and I felt sad because it was almost like seeing the demise of a living creature.

When the marine harbourmaster retired the local boat owners prepared a special day for him. The owners of the largest yacht took him out for a day's sailing and on their return every boat, large and small, assembled opposite our house. I knew many of the owners and they waved to me as I watched from the terrace. When the yacht appeared they all greeted it with sirens and escorted the harbourmaster back to the marina. It was quite a sight and those of us ashore waved as they passed.

One day I heard a low-flying helicopter and as it came into view over the sea, I could see that it was in trouble. It got lower and lower – I was convinced it was going to crash. Finally, it landed safely on an open space on a nearby headland. Apparently it was almost out of fuel and stayed there for half the day while fuel was brought from the airport. The local children were delighted.

Over the years *The Archers* have taken part in several *Songs of Praise* and one that I remember with great pleasure took place in the Balearic Islands. Sir Harry Secombe, complete with director, sound and camera crews, came over to Casa Ruisenor. An interview was shot as he and I sat on my terrace overlooking the sea.

It was lovely to meet and work with someone who had made me laugh so much and whose beautiful singing voice I had long admired. 'You often sing to me here,' I told him. When he looked puzzled I fetched one of my tapes of operatic arias with Callas, Domingo, Carreras . . . and Secombe. 'Oh,' he said, 'I'm in good company!'

He sang to me again on another island when I was invited to be the castaway on Radio 4's *Desert Island Discs*. I chose his singing for one of my eight gramophone records. 'The Stars Were Brightly Shining' from *Tosca* by Puccini. What struck me most on meeting him was his innate goodness. Here, I felt, was a really good man. Together with the crew, we had lunch together at a restaurant in the village and later they flew back to Majorca. It was lucky we finished filming by lunchtime – there was a power cut all afternoon!

I have since then been interviewed by the charming and talented presenter, Aled Jones, for two more *Songs of Praise*. One for Harvest Festival for which I went to the church in Eversham, and for the Valentine's Day programme Aled and the crew came to my home for the interview. They also shot scenes in our church and at Roger's graveside.

Sadly, we have lost many of our cast members through death. Some were re-cast – we had four Dan Archers and two Walter Gabriels. The first Walter, Robert Maudsley, died quite early on, as far as I remember from a brain tumour. At first, listeners would not accept Chriss Gittins in his place. Poor Chriss – such a sweet, gentle man, it nearly broke his heart! But he won through in the end and his Walter became a greatly loved character.

I suppose Norman Painting's death has affected me most. When we first met at the Region's studio he was a young man just down from Oxford and destined for an academic career, for which he was very well qualified. Yet somehow, through writing for radio and then being drawn into acting, it took over and his career changed course. Little did he realise then that he was destined to become a household name as Philip Archer or that he would be the actor playing the same role for the greatest length of time.

Although he and I became the last two surviving actors from the pilot week of *The Archers*, I had not played Peggy without a break. That came when Roger and I adopted our two children (of which more in the next chapter), but I was soon back again playing Rita.

Norman and I acted in many shows together for Children's Hour, some of which he had written and also composed the music and appeared in a variety of other programmes as well. He wrote many of *The Archers'* scripts at the same time as acting in them. A man of many talents, he was also a keen and knowledgeable gardener. He once told me that two of his roses were 'Mrs P' and 'Old Walter'. With a mischievous grin he added: 'I've put them in the bed together!' More than once he invited the whole cast and their children to picnic in his garden and swim in the indoor pool.

Thirty or so years ago Norman was feeling rather stressed out so we invited him, along with a cousin of mine, to stay with us in Menorca and gave him space to relax. He decided one day that he would like to go off on his own to explore the island a bit more. Being no bus service out of the village, he assured us that he would hitch lifts. It was before the days of mobile phones, so I was a bit concerned that he would not be able to contact me to go and collect him if he got stranded, but he was determined to be independent and so off he went. He didn't come back for lunch or tea and by eight o'clock we were getting anxious until a taxi drew up outside and deposited a slightly unsteady Norman.

It seems he had fallen in with a van driver delivering to just about every bar on the island and at every port of call they received a little 'refreshment'. They ended up in Mahon, where he had picked up the taxi.

'You must be very hungry,' I said. 'Would you like a meal now?'

'No, thank you,' he replied, 'I think I'll just go to bed.' And we didn't see him again till morning!

While Norman was staying with us he wrote a poem, a copy of which hangs on the wall of the bedroom he occupied – so we can add 'Poet' to all his other talents. Here is that poem, echoing Keats' 'Ode to a Nightingale':

The world ends here: the day's perplexities
Slip like the spray that veils the distant rocks
Back to the element that flings it up.
Safe as the sea, contentment lingers here:
A place of saints and laughter, friends and clowns,

Of hoopoes, cats and little busy dogs,
Bee-eaters, kites – such wealth of birds and flowers,
Sea creatures, butterflies, white houses, wrinkled crags
The island shimmers with their light and life,
With calm and balm and healing for the soul
Peace for the spirit, order for the mind.
Unlocked by love, the magic casements open
On seas not perilous and not forlorn,
Rock rose and rosemary and sweet wild rose,
Heathers and herbs foam over faery lands,
Where all the time a nightingale seems singing.
Somewhere just out of sight near Macaret.

There could never be another Doris or Mrs P and Denis Folwell's voice as Jack was too distinctive to be followed. That said, Edgar Harrison (Dan number three) gave an incredible impersonation of Denis's voice after he had died when a telephone call from Jack to Peggy shortly before Jack's death was needed. To hear that voice again was such an emotional experience for me that I was glad we did it in one take – I only just made it to the privacy of the ladies' before I broke down.

It has not always been plain sailing for me. Both in the theatre and in radio an actress can be called upon to scream. In my rep days I was in a play that called for me to scream off-stage. I stood in the wings, having a whispered conversation with the young juvenile, but listening for my cue. When it came and I emitted a blood-curdling scream, the poor man nearly jumped out of his skin: 'I didn't touch her!' he protested.

Amusing, but over the years and after a lot more screaming in radio thriller serials, I was beginning to have trouble with my voice. It was becoming husky, even breaking in some registers. I began to fear something might be wrong and my doctor referred me to a throat specialist. I was so afraid I might have to give up the work I loved.

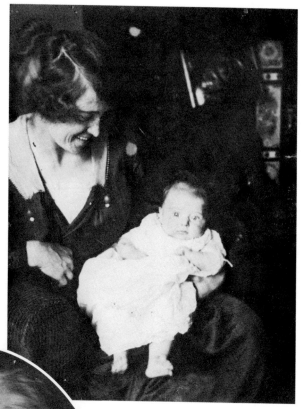

photoshoot with Mother: 'Great big
and a lot of fuzz on to top.' Photo
by my father.

Aged 2 years 10 months. I wasn't as
angelic as I looked!

With Leslie and Douglas Cox outside 30 Bingham Road, Nottingham, my birthplace.

Centre: Glamour girl in 1946. By now I was in London and getting lots of lovely radio work.

As Emily in *Milestones* for the Nottingham Repertory Theatre, 1943.

ur wedding, 27 May 1942. From left to right: Roger's parents, Captain Frank Ladner (best man), oger's cheeky grin, the seven guinea wedding dress, my father, Roger's sister Beryl and Mum.

Peggy and Jack Archer, washing eggs, 1951. The things we do for our art!

My 'Rita Flynn' days – and lots of other things too.

Roger and me out on the town. What a handsome pair!

My friend Helen with me in her garden.

Princess Ann when she came to open Pebble Mill studios. Norman Painting, me, Gwen Berryman and Tony Shryane. I can't remember what the joke was but it must have been a good one!

A magazine photographer had called to photograph me but Pippin insisted on getting in on the act.

David and Deborah with my parents at the time of their diamond wedding. David and Deb were just married.

Proud grandparents: Roger, me, Claire. You can't believe how a funny little baby could grow into such a beautiful girl.

Proud grandad on a visit to Germany.

David and Deborah in their pas de deux, 'Winter' in *The Four Seasons* ballet.

The last photo of David and Roz, summer 2006.

Rozzy and Ros – my happy girls.

rchers Addicts: at Losely Park with Edward Kelsey as Joe Grundy and Arnold Peters who plays Jack. hat was the day the wasp stung me on my bottom.

a the occasion of Chris Gittins' 80th birthday. Bob Arnold, me, Patricia Greene, Norman Painting d Chris.

All set in my bulldozer and ready to 'brin[g]
down the house'!

My favourite photo of Roger and me outside our retirement bungalow in Surrey. Retirement for Rog[er]
– but not for me!

With Graham Gauld in Menorca.

In Menorca with Smoky, Voodoo and Flurry.

hristmas in Menorca on our rrace with Bob and Josie. This volved setting the camera up in y bedroom window and then shing out in time for the photo. I ade it!

Roger with Pickles who was advising Roger on his game.

Dear Nora, staunch friend and helper.

With Flurry – wasn't he adorable?!

Jack and Peggy's wedding day, 1991. At the reception – with the cake!

rnold Peters as Jack Woolley and me as eggy with the Ambridge Rose at the helsea Flower Show, 1990.

At Buckingham Palace, OBE day, 1991. Who said I wouldn't get anywhere without my school certificate

Receiving a *Daily Mail* award on behalf of *The Archers*. He was rather a dish, wasn't he!

The cast party after Jack and Peggy's wedding, 1991. Front row: Colin Skipp (Tony), Mollie Harris (Martha), Patricia Greene (Jill), Arnold Peters (Jack), me, Margot Boyd (Mrs Antrobus) and Judy Bennett (Shula). Sitting on the floor: Louiza Patikas (Helen) and Felicity Finch (Ruth).

The Archers at my 90th birthday party in 2009. Arnold Peters (Jack), Vanessa Whitburn (Archers editor), Judy Bennett (Shula) Charles Collingwood (Brian), unknown man, Liz Rigby (past editor) Patricia Greene (Jill), Edward Kelsey (Joe), me, Colin Skipp (Tony), John Pierce (retired engineer) Hedi Niklaus (Kathy), Alaric Cotter (actor and producer), Val Fidler (past senior assistant).

My wonderful day at the Guildhall to receive the Freedom of the City of London, seen here with the Lord Mayor of London, Nicholas Anstee.

Nodules on my vocal chords were diagnosed, a condition often suffered by singers and actors. Thankfully he did not suggest operating. It is an operation often performed but not always successfully and in the case of Julie Andrews, it went disastrously wrong and her beautiful singing voice was lost.

The specialist thought my case could be cured by therapy so I embarked on the long, hard grind to recovery. Every day I shut myself away with a tape recorder and worked on the exercises I had been given. For many months I didn't seem to be making much progress and I became very depressed, all the while doing every trick I could think of to nurse my voice through the scenes when working.

'It's no better,' I would tell Roger in despair and as ever, he gave me his full support and encouragement. Eventually the nodules reduced and disappeared. Now my voice is lower than years ago and my singing voice has gone altogether but at least I'm still able to work.

It is quite feasible Peggy's voice would become deeper with age and for any rough edges I have my great stand-by: honey water. I take it into the studio with me, where I am teased because the others pretend to think it's really whisky! I hate whisky, but I don't mind being teased.

If one of the cast is suffering from a bad cold (and it shows) then an extra line may be added, commenting on the fact – we have to be really ill before we let the show down and stay at home. As you can imagine, it causes so much upheaval, with writers having to be summoned to do rewrites, covering the character's absence.

• Chapter 9 •

Adoption and Holidays

For reasons that I won't go into here Roger and I decided to complete our family by way of adoption. I longed for children and by the time we moved into our first house in Worcester Park, we were both over 30. It was high time to do it.

Having gone on the waiting list with Surrey County Council, it was almost a year before we had news of a little boy and drove to the nursery in Hindhead, where he was being cared for. Blond and beautiful, he was 10 months old and had been just a few days old when he had arrived at the nursery, with not much hope of survival. By the time we saw him he was robust, though, and sat quite happily on my knee. After that we visited him each weekend and I also went down midweek to take him out in his pram, feed and bath him and put him to bed. By the time he was almost a year old he was used to me looking after him.

It didn't seem right to bring a baby into a strange environment and then go off to Birmingham and leave him so I resigned from

The Archers and the late Thelma Rogers took over as Peggy until I returned. Jack and Peggy were just about to take on the management of The Bull and Denis (Jack) was not best pleased with me, to say the least. Robert Mawdesley, the original Walter, comforted me, saying: 'Adopt your baby and be happy.' It was so sad that Robert died soon afterwards.

David clearly missed the matron of the nursery, who had nursed him and been the only mother figure he had ever known, and he cried for her. I know his sad 'Mama' was for her, not me and I was finding it hard to win his love. But in the end we won through and a strong and loving bond between us lasted until his death, so many years later.

On the beach one day when he was two an elderly lady smiled at him. He gestured to Roger and me, then said: 'That's my mummy, that's my daddy.' Our hearts were so full of happiness.

Two years later we were ready for the next instalment. The first time we visited little Ros, aged 10 months, at a different nursery she howled the whole time. Oh dear, we thought, she doesn't seem to like us! However, a few days later I went down again, taking a plastic toy. I sat on a low stool and dangled it from my finger without saying anything to her. She clearly remembered me and, with her funny way of sitting with one leg tucked underneath her, edged back and forth, getting nearer to me each time until she could grab the toy and retreat with it. It was like taming a bird, I thought.

After that there were no more problems and we took David down to meet her. He had been very interested in the preparations for her coming and confided in my mother: 'I think baby sister come soon.'

The date was arranged to collect her and I had accordingly turned down the lead in a six-part serial when – disaster! I received a phone call to say that the nursery was in quarantine and she couldn't leave. Nevertheless I was able to persuade Matron that I would take full responsibility for her and with her agreement, I went down and brought her home. The next day I had a phone call from the children's department saying they understood I was willing to take full responsibility and therefore they would agree to us bringing the child home. Little Ros was at that moment sitting on the floor at my feet and grinning up at me – I've always told her that we kidnapped her.

Ros settled in with no problems. She adored David and he treated her with great affection. In every photo of them together he is holding her hand. On their first night in the nursery, David in his small bed and Ros in her cot, I tucked them up and then listened outside the door. Ros was making contented little noises and after a few moments came David's firm voice: 'You be quiet,' he told her – and she was.

For the first six months in each case we were technically fostering and during that time the birth parents can ask for their child to be returned to them. Thank goodness that didn't happen! The next six months we were on probation, with visits from a very pleasant social worker – '*Guardian Ad Litem*' – who went with us each time for the adoption ceremonies in Judges' Chambers. This, of course, was a red-letter day: now they were well and truly ours and our little family was complete!

Watching the children's personalities and characters develop was fascinating. We could not expect them to take after us, even though they shared our environment, but it soon emerged that Ros had traits in common with Roger – her practicality, no-nonsense attitude to life and stoicism plus the way she managed her 'finances' from an early age. If a visiting relative gave them half a crown each, Ros would buy a six-penny savings stamp, a posy of flowers for me and spend what was left on herself. David, on the other hand, would blow the lot on a toy. For his entire life he was quite unable to keep out of debt. In that he was unlike me, otherwise we had so much in common. We laughed so much at the same sort of things, often to the bewilderment of Roger and Ros.

I could see a love of music developing from a very early age and a great tendency to dramatise things. Looking back, it seems inevitable David's future career would be in the theatre, though totally unexpected at the time. He had emotional difficulties all his life and caught every childish ailment going, so his school attendance was constantly being interrupted. Measles, whooping cough, scarlet fever, pneumonia, mumps and chicken pox . . . the last two he passed onto Ros and me. ('Oh Mummy, you look like Humpty Dumpty!') And believe me, chicken pox is not something you want to have in adulthood.

Ros had her own names for certain things. A multi-storey car park became 'a multi-stilo car park', while windscreen wipers were 'wind-scripes' – which I still find myself using, more often than not.

As a very small girl Ros was always interested in the scripture lessons and according to her school report: 'Rosalind often has a comment to make' (I wonder what they were). And I would hear her coming home from school, open hymn book in hand and singing, 'Alle, alle-oola', so it naturally followed that she would go to Sunday school, until one day when she announced that she would not be going.

Surprised, I said: 'I thought you liked Sunday school.'

'Oh, I do,' she replied, 'but I've given it up for Lent.'

There's no answer to that! Which reminds me of the time when my mother was living with us and it was the Tuesday before Easter . . .

She said brightly, 'Pancakes today!'

'No, Mum,' I told her, 'I'm afraid you missed them this year because I was away working.'

'No,' she said, 'Shrove Tuesday, Ash Wednesday, Maundy Thursday, Good Friday.'

'What happened to Lent?' I asked.

To which she replied: 'Oh, we've had that.'

So I made her pancakes.

When the children were small I wasn't accepting very much work. I took them for a month's holiday in Mudeford. One of my uncles owned a beach hut there, which we were able to borrow. We also rented a (not very well) converted stable a very short way from the beach. Roger came down at weekends. Invariably we had a spell of cold, wet weather and so I went out and bought an electric fire to cheer up that cold and dismal place.

One evening, having got the children to bed, I settled down with the *Radio Times* to find something to listen to. Soon I noticed an article about a play in verse that I had acted in several years before. I read: 'The part of Margaret, brilliantly played by June Spencer in the earlier production, will be played by . . .' – and I sat down on the floor and cried.

I loved the children dearly and they came first with me – but oh I did miss my old, fuller career! When an actor is 'unavailable' for any length of time it is extremely difficult to get back into the swim again.

Reggie Smith once tried to persuade me to join the BBC Repertory Company but at that time it was not possible to accommodate rep and *The Archers*. After due thought I decided to stay with *The Archers* – and how right I was!

The children just accepted that I would often go off and 'be' someone else on the radio. Indeed, David was quite blasé about it from a very early age. One day Roger settled down with him to listen to me on Children's Hour. After a while David decided he'd rather be in the garden. 'Don't you want to stay and listen to Mummy?' asked Roger. David's reply was to toddle up to the radio, give it a little wave and say: 'Bye-bye, Mummy.' He then went off into the garden.

Ros, when about 10, said: 'I don't know! One minute you're here with us, the next you're off as Penny, having adventures with Steve.'

Watching the film *Little Women* with my two children one day, the following exchange took place:

David: Why are they crying?

Me: Because their mother's got to go away.

Ros: (with great scorn) *We* don't cry when you go to Birmingham.

David: No, we help you on your way!

So much for missing me . . .

Only once did I make the mistake of leaving them without supervision. It was the school holidays and they somehow persuaded me that they could manage perfectly well on their own. I was only going to London for a short recording and would be gone for about four hours, so I left lunch for them and later rang home to see how they were getting on. They sounded rather excited. It appears they had been playing water games and had flooded the bathroom floor. Water had gone through into the light fitting in the downstairs cloakroom; it also permeated the kitchen ceiling, the paper of which was sagging.

'Don't touch *anything*! Just phone Grandad and ask him to come,' I shouted.

Having read them the riot act on my return, things calmed down until late that night when I went into the bathroom and shut the door. In the door were two enormous dents. I went out onto the landing, shouting, 'Everybody up!' Out came two sleepy-eyed children: 'Who did that?' 'It was Ros!' 'How?' 'With her knees.'

A wet rubber floor is apparently just the thing for sliding on at top speed but I've never been able to understand how little Ros's knees were tougher than the door.

I was not altogether surprised when one babysitter – a nice elderly woman – informed me that our two were the naughtiest children she had ever known, but I hung my head all the same. They were just so full of high spirits, but at least they were happy and the bond between them closer than many natural siblings.

Shortly after the war Roger and I had gone by sea to Brittany and stayed at a faded grand hotel on the beach at St Lunaire. We thought it would be an ideal place to bring our children in the future. When David was five and Ros only three we flew to Dinard, landing in what was virtually a field. David gazed about him and passed judgement: 'This isn't much of a place.'

We walked into a large shed, where we collected our luggage and walked out past a very tall gendarme. Little Ros assumed he must be our host. Gazing up at him, she offered her hand and said: 'Thank you for the ride.' He looked delighted and I'm sure it made his day.

St Lunaire was just as we'd remembered it except the hotel was now converted into flats and we were staying at the village inn, where the accommodation was a bit primitive but the food was superb. Every night, with the children in bed, we would adjourn to the bar and work our way along the row of liqueurs after dinner. Just the one each night! Eventually we came to a mauve-coloured one called 'Parfait Amour'. It was very good. The next night Roger told me: 'You're not having that one again!' He always had a lovely, dry wit.

We had a delightful trip up the River Rance to Dinan. The many starving cats there had most of my packed lunch! On the journey back, the country bus packed with ducks and chickens was quite an experience. That whole holiday was reminiscent of *Monsieur Hulot's Holiday*.

When David was about seven I took him to see *Mon Oncle*. The humour appealed to him and he chuckled his way through it. He had a great sense of humour. Conversely he could be moved to tears by a film. In later years, when he was a teenager, we saw *West Side Story* more than once. Both he and I had to wipe our eyes as the credits rolled.

Ros's polite thanks to the gendarme reminded me of collecting her from a party at which the parting gift for each child was rather oddly a plastic sponge and a bath cube. Her parting words to her hostess were: 'Thank you for the present. Actually, I don't use them but I can always give them to Daddy for the car!'

We had some happy holidays with the children, some of necessity costing very little money while Roger climbed the civilian ladder, starting at the lowest rung after the war. A farm holiday in the Gower Peninsula was a bit of a challenge, though. Roger and I were expected to help with the harvest. My job was to stuff holes in the sacks with straw to prevent grain escaping. David had to bring the geese down to the farm for the night. Ros helped the farmer bring the cow to be milked, but to this day she insists it was Biddy the bull!

At one point Roger had to go off in the car to visit a firm's client, so I collected a tarpaulin and some string plus a packed lunch and marched the children in single file the half mile to the beach. I took one look at the clouds and despatched them to the beach to find big pieces of driftwood to make a shelter. With those for a frame, spanning a gap in the sand hills and the tarpaulin over the top, we entered our little shelter just as the rain began.

Unfortunately, with the rain came a sudden change in wind direction. It blew the rain directly onto us. 'Keep close to me!' I ordered. Lifting the tarpaulin, we scuttled underneath it to the other side of the sand hills, where we spent the rest of the day before walking back to the farm. I thought it was all great fun. Not so David, who greeted Roger with: 'Oh Daddy, I'm so glad you're back with the car – it's been *awful!*'

Another break in the Isle of Wight brought better weather. David and I went to the stables and had a couple of pleasant rides. As I had not ridden for about 20 years, I asked for a quiet mount. They handed me a stout stick, saying, 'You'll need this.' The first thing my four-footed friend did was to stroll up to an unsuspecting man and bite a button off his jacket! Then we were off, David at the front on a leading rein. I soon realised what the stick was for: I was always last going through the gates and sometimes my horse didn't want to go through at all. Acutely embarrassed, David called: 'Kick him, Mummy!' 'I am doing,' I replied. The next time we went out I said I hadn't meant quite so quiet, so I was given a real goer and we led the pack. I haven't ridden since and David soon switched to dancing while Ros rode instead.

I used to take her for lessons at an indoor school and watch from the balcony as the little girls on Thelwell ponies took instruction from a very superior young lady. I used to wait for it: 'Pwepare to twot – ter-wot!'

We took it in turns to watch the children on the beach. David would head for the nearest cliff and little Ros's target was always the sea. She would crawl into it from day one, like a newly hatched turtle. While we were swimming, she would bob about with us on a rubber ring. Later, she queried over lunch one holiday: 'Please can I have a guggle and snorter?' Finally, we worked out what it was she wanted: goggles and snorkel. She would swim along happily, with contented humming noises coming up through the snorkel.

It's amazing how much embarrassment two small children can inflict on their unsuspecting parents. The hotel in which we stayed in Guernsey rashly offered baby-sitting facilities and assured us there would be no problem in leaving our five- and three-year-old in bed while we took an evening off.

Arriving back at about 10pm we found the other residents being entertained in the lounge by our two in pyjamas and dressing gowns. We gathered it was all going very well and they had been highly entertaining. What family secrets, we wondered, were now public knowledge?

On another occasion, this time in a hotel in Menorca, Roger and I were on our way down to dinner in the lift when it ground to a halt between floors. It was quite some time before help came and there was about 18 inches through which we could see the foyer. After a short while we found we were being peered at by what appeared to be all the children who were staying in the hotel. In the centre were our two, clearly the organisers of the sightseeing tour, proudly explaining that we were their parents and inviting them all to have a good laugh at our expense!

They were both strong swimmers. David had a graceful crawl – everything he did was elegant! Ros passed her mile test and also the test for lifesaving. She gave me quite a scare by swimming straight out to sea one evening. We arrived on the hotel terrace and someone pointed to a dot way out to sea, with the words, 'That's your daughter.' Someone else handed me a pair of binoculars and I focused on the bobbing head. At that moment she turned and sure enough, it was Ros with a broad grin on her face! She had achieved what she set out to do: to swim out until she was level with the headland.

The children were always very enterprising on holiday. They weren't content just to spend money – they weren't averse to making a bit for themselves too. It wasn't until many years later when they owned up to it that I found out about the following exploit. I strongly suspect Ros was the brains behind the scheme – she was always canny in planning her financial affairs whereas David was a victim of insolvency all his life. I was greatly shocked to hear that in Majorca, when they were both under 10, they discovered that a soft drinks shop would pay money for empties. Our two would collect bottles, take them in, collect on them and then at a later date, collect them from the rear of the store where the shopkeeper kept them and take them in again! 'But that was dishonest!' I said. Of course, it was many years too late to read them the riot act.

Another time they went through Customs and insisted on declaring 400 lolly sticks that they had collected, much to the amusement of the officer on duty. Many of those were cleverly recycled and presented at Christmas time as plant potholders. That same holiday they tried to bring home a tiny kitten. When we explained that it wasn't possible because of quarantine regulations they tearfully insisted: 'It will be drowned if we can't save it.' How I wished we could have taken it home, but I didn't think Candy, our own cat, would have approved.

I was never a good swimmer – I swam the breaststroke in an almost perpendicular position like a seahorse in an effort to keep my head above water. This meant that although I didn't make much progress, at least I got a lot of exercise. The children would swim alongside me, creating noises like a steam engine and making remarks about the *Queen Mary* until I laughed so much that I nearly went under.

I would only swim if the sea was flat calm and one day, on a crowded beach, it was so rough there was no question of my swimming. Instead I thought it would be fun to stand at the water's edge and let the waves dash over me. After a bit came the big seventh wave and I braced myself to meet it.

I was just priding myself on still being on my feet when I noticed a man a few feet away, smiling at me in a rather quizzical manner. To my horror I realised my bikini bottom was draped round my ankles! Luckily he didn't have a camera and I managed to pull it up before the whole beach noticed.

It brought back a memory of when I was teenager and knitted myself a smart red swimsuit. All was well until I went in for a swim. After a few moments I thought my legs had become entangled in seaweed but soon found it was my swimsuit, stretched beyond recall. I had to call for a towel before I could come out of the water!

We always had to be prepared for the unexpected when on holiday with Ros. She once caused a hush in a Menorcan hotel dining room by getting her finger stuck in the top of a wine bottle. Don't ask me how she managed it, but she only found she could remove it when the waiter threatened to smash the bottle. She went one better in Ibiza, though. We climbed to the top of the hill only to find the massive door to the cathedral locked. Yes, you've guessed it – Ros got her finger stuck in the keyhole!

I'm not sure if I believe her story of getting her finger stuck in a knothole in the floor at her boarding school so they had to take a saw to the floorboards but we were very proud of her one fiesta time when she entered the children's swimming competition. The only girl among a crowd of boys, she powered her way down the pool to excited shouts from all the parents. A French woman shouted, '*C'est la fille!*' (It's the girl!) – and so it was. She won a bottle of champagne and was photographed proudly holding it. I don't think she was keen on champagne at that time – but we enjoyed it.

David's last holiday *en famille* was in Ibiza. At 17 he was very popular with the girls and we saw very little of him during the day. When it was time to leave we boarded the bus to take us to the airport. There seemed to be a big turnout: women of all ages, little girls and chambermaids. I was feeling a bit surprised by the attention we were getting until the bus began to move and a female chorus went up: 'Goodbye, David,' they said, with sad faces.

Oh David, no wonder we hadn't seen much of you!

• Chapter 10 •
Brief Thoughts on Fashion and Cooking

With my love of pretty clothes the war and rationing was a challenge to my ingenuity. I made a fetching négligée out of curtain net (which wasn't rationed) and Roger sent silk from India; also a jungle-green thin blanket, which made a warm housecoat – very useful in my under-heated bedsit during the cold winter months.

The instant that the rationing of clothes ceased, fashion swung the other way and we rejoiced in the longer, fuller skirts of the New Look. I was into it 100 per cent and went around looking like Little Bo Peep. In those days I was very much a hat person – I loved them. I had one hat that I called 'The Burmese Temple' and another was 'The Cream Puff'.

David always took a keen interest in my clothes and he had perfect taste so his comments were worth paying attention to. When he was no more than six, I bought a red hat, which I thought I could wear with a red dress that I already had. David's remark was: 'Oh Mummy, your hat nearly matches your dress!' After that, I never wore them together again.

On another occasion he was even more succinct. Watching me put on my latest purchase, he said: 'That's new.' 'Yes, I bought it this morning.' After quite a long pause he said: 'I'm not laughing.' I went right off that hat!

With the Swinging Sixties up went hemlines and Denis Folwell (Jack Archer) remarked that it was the first time he'd seen my legs. When our son David came home on holiday from Germany he said privately to Roger, 'Aren't Mum's skirts a bit short?' And to me he observed: 'Isn't Dad's hair a bit long?'

It is the constant worry of the young that their parents should not breach the bounds of propriety hence the anxiety of making sure they won't let you down and make idiots of themselves at school functions by not turning up (to their minds) suitably and soberly dressed. I have often marvelled at the coincidence of David getting stuck up a tree when I was wearing a tight skirt and winklepickers so that it was extremely difficult to climb up to guide him safely down.

Winklepickers, by the way, were high-heeled shoes with long pointed toes, rather like the ones the young are wearing now. I long to go up to them and tell them shoes like that ruined my feet so that now I can only wear 'sensible' – i.e. dowdy – ones. It wouldn't make the slightest difference, I know, for the young never believe they'll ever be old.

David and trees were a constant hazard. I once had a phone call from the mother of one of his playmates: 'David's just fallen out of a tree in our garden but don't worry, he's all right.' Being a mother exposes you to some strange requests. For example: 'Mummy, can you come. There's a toad stuck in the spout of the watering can!' I solved that one by turning the tap on hard down the narrow end and blasting it out into the can.

Numerous times Roger would arrive home from the office to find a note: Taken David/Ros to hospital. Need stitches. Dinner in oven! I always suspect they asked me to open the new extension to the cottage hospital because we were their best customers.

Unlike my radio daughter Jennifer, who in her real-life persona of Angela Piper writes splendid cookery books, my culinary efforts are of a more slapdash variety. When entertaining I can produce a pretty good Coq au Vin, Spaghetti alla Bolognese and Boeuf Bourguignon and I'm famed for my Crêpes Suzettes. It is the result of extreme effort and concentration, something that cannot possibly be sustained in everyday living.

Mother taught me how to be a good plain cook but she had no adventure in her menus. My first effort to toss a pancake landed it draped over the back-door key and until we invested in a toaster, Roger said he always knew when breakfast was ready because he could smell the toast burning.

Roger was very fond of Christmas pudding and at my first attempt suggested we might need more than one, so we did three times the recipe instructions. We started by breaking 15 eggs into a bowl and went on from there. When we had filled every pudding basin in the house and still seemed to have as much again left, I got the car out, drove down to my parents' and borrowed all theirs – just as well Christmas puddings keep.

The first time my in-laws came to spend the festive season with us was also the first time that I had ever cooked a complete Christmas dinner on my own. It was planned and timed down to the last detail, with lists for everything. By some miracle everything was cooked and ready at the appointed time. I was congratulating myself with huge relief and putting all the saucepans in to soak when my mother-in-law came to inspect the kitchen. In a withering voice she said: 'Is *that* how you leave your sink?' It was all too much and I burst into tears.

My parents, on the other hand, were like a couple of kids when they came and enjoyed everything. I think I must hold the record for burning saucepans. It would never do for me to have a smoke alarm – it would be going off all the time! People tell me I should have one in case there is a fire in the night. Once I've taken my hearing aids out, I shouldn't hear it anyway.

One of the most interesting of my cooking disasters took place in Menorca. I put some eggs on to hard-boil, ready for a light lunch of egg mayonnaise. A little later I went out to do the shopping with the friend staying with me. We had a leisurely coffee and were debating whether or not to go for a little drive before returning home, when suddenly I said: 'Oh no, I forgot to turn the eggs off!'

We could smell them as soon as we reached the end of the road. You would not believe what a lot of ground four eggs can cover . . . and walls . . . and ceiling. For days after we were finding bits of mummified eggs. I threw that saucepan away. My friend said at least there was never a dull moment holidaying with me.

Talking of Boeuf Bourguignon, as I was a moment ago, reminds me of when I took Ros to Paris to celebrate her eighteenth birthday. We saw it on the menu and I thought this is bound to be special in its country of origin. What a disappointment! It was a plain, beef stew. 'Boeuf Bourguignon, my foot!' I exclaimed in disgust and to this day that is what Ros always calls it.

At another small restaurant, on that same holiday, Ros and I were enjoying a delicious terrine when in came a very British mother, father and two children. Mother took charge.

'What's this?' she asked, pointing to the menu.

'Terrine,' said the waitress, 'It is a sort of meat pie.'

'Right,' said Mother, 'we'll have four meat pies, we'll forget all this . . . and did I see some gâteau cake?'

Chapter 11

Changing Times

First Geoffrey Webb and then Ted Mason – our scriptwriters – died, then Norman Painting, who under the guise of Bruno Milna scripted the programmes as well as playing Phil. Since then we have had numerous scriptwriters and editors. Most of the latter were good to work for and with the two exceptions I kept my head below the parapet until they went away!

Peggy's character suffered many years of confusion. Each writer seemed to have a different concept of her and at times she had a personality change from week to week. She went from being a sensible businesswoman who had run The Bull and later Grey Gables to an empty-headed incompetent; from an unpleasant gossip to a caring family member – and once she was written as a snooty 'county' lady, forgetting that she was Mrs P's daughter from an East End background. Paddy Greene once said: 'Poor Peggy, she's going through the change – of scriptwriter!'

At that time the Sunday Omnibus edition of *The Archers* had to be slightly condensed to fit into the allotted time – less than the sum of the five daily episodes – and if an actor was edited out, he didn't receive his repeat fee. Each Sunday Philip Garston-Jones, the first Jack Woolley, would sit by his radio with the week's scripts to check who had lost out. He would then report to us how many 'repeats' each of us had lost.

When Philip collapsed one day it was wrongly reported on air that he had died. The following week he did indeed die and so it was again broadcast on the news. I could almost hear him saying: 'I got my repeat.'

The Omnibus now doesn't need to be cut. With Philip's death, Jack Woolley had to be recast and the role went to Arnold Peters, with whom I worked many times in the Midland Region. At first it inevitably felt strange but Arnold's 'Brummy' was so good that we soon fell into an easy working relationship and I cannot imagine anyone bettering his performance as Jack sinks into dementia: such a difficult challenge for an actor and so beautifully and movingly done.

In the early years of *The Archers* we had a number of real countrymen playing the roles of the Ambridge locals. These were folk untrained in the art of acting but with a wealth of experience in radio work, in which they virtually played themselves. Bob Arnold was the most central of these, playing Tom Forrest. I worked with him in features (programmes about a specific subject or theme) and Children's Hour, always playing a countryman or old Crusty the gardener in *Through the Garden Gate*. For many years it was his warm, country voice that introduced *The Archers Omnibus* on Sunday mornings.

Another hilarious character was Ned Larkin, played by Bill Payne. Bill was an irrepressible comic who became so totally immersed in his role that he lived it 24 hours a day. One day I came out of New Street Station in Birmingham on my way to the studio, where I was confronted with a news placard: 'Archers Star

Dies'. Worrying which of my friends it was, I found it was Bill. He too had been on his way to the studio.

When that sort of tragedy strikes the whole production staff have to work through their sadness to keep things going. At very short notice, scriptwriters are summoned to write out the character and the storyline kept going through the words of other characters. A recent case was that of Norman Painting when it was decided that Phil should be allowed to celebrate Christmas. It would have been doubly sad for him to die during the festive season so he was kept 'alive' by hearsay until the right time was found for a gentle death.

Another old trouper who completed her day's recording and then collapsed and died on leaving the building was Mary Wimbush, with whom I had worked since her very first broadcast. It was a great shock to us all but what a way to go! I hope I can work to the end.

Molly Harris was another country character and she always came to the studio wearing a fresh bloom from her garden. When we eventually attended her funeral, we all wore a flower in her memory.

It was at this time that there were rumblings in the cast about using 'amateur' actors who were not members of Equity, the actor's trade union. As the old actors faded away, professionals experienced in playing all kinds of dialects followed in their wake.

Veteran broadcaster Chriss Gittins (Walter Gabriel) was totally reliable in the studio, but outside even he would admit to being accident-prone. He had a scar, which he told me he had long ago sustained in a ballroom.

'Oh dear,' I said, 'what happened to your partner?'

'Oh, I wasn't dancing,' said Chriss, 'I was putting up coloured lights, got a shock and fell off the ladder.'

Then there was the time when he and his wife May, returning from a holiday on the continent, missed the ferry back to

England and put up for the night at a small hotel. While May had gone to the bathroom, Chriss was intrigued by a very ancient wardrobe, which was nailed shut. Curious as to what might be inside, he forced it open and stepped inside to retrieve an old sock, which appeared to be the only thing there. The next thing he knew, he was lying flat on the bed with the wardrobe on top of him! And this was the sight that met May's eyes on her return.

After May died he came with friends to stay with me in Menorca. He asked to borrow a brush and dustpan to sweep up some sand on his bedroom floor. As we were beginning to wonder why he was so long, there came a plaintive voice: 'Can someone come and help me put my door back on its hinges?' In lifting it to get a bit of grit from underneath, he'd gone a bit too far and found he couldn't get it back on again!

Chriss was quite high up in the hierarchy of the Scouting Movement and he invited Roger and me to be his guests at Windsor Castle for a big event. It was a beautiful hot summer's day and inevitably one of the younger scouts fainted in the heat. On came two scouts bearing a stretcher and very efficiently loaded the prostrate body onto it. There the efficiency ground to a halt for they picked up the stretcher and set off, both with the intention of leading the way. Back to back, it almost became a tug of war – they got it right in the end.

In the early days of *The Archers* we were a very small cast and were called upon to 'double' a number of minor roles in addition to our own principal parts. My main 'double' was Rita Flynn, the Irish girl who worked for Doughy Hood in the bakery. Her reason for being in Ambridge was that she had been there during the war as a Land Girl and had stayed on.

Another major 'double' was the formidable Mrs Spenlow. She came about by accident. An elderly actress was taken ill and was unable to get to the studio one day so I was asked to take her lines, but as a new character. I confess Mrs Spenlow owed a lot to Dame Edith Evans as Lady Bracknell but the scriptwriters (one of whom was Norman Painting at that time) liked her so much that she became a regular, laying down the law and complaining about the mud on the roads caused by the farming methods of the Grundys.

Another character was the Tregorran's maid. I used my Scottish voice for her. On one occasion I announced, 'Mrs Peggy Archer to see you, M'am' – then quickly stepped back a few paces and made my entrance as Peggy! I played Jennifer as a child and also uttered Tony's first word, regrettably 'Ta'.

Nowadays the cast members are called on to double if only the odd line is needed. For anything bigger, a new actor is called in and so the cast of characters consistently evolves.

Like anyone else, actors can have health problems and if they are unable to work, a suitable storyline has to cover for a long absence. The late Norman Painting was a case in point. A strong central character, he had many years of ill health, including an operation for a quadruple heart bypass. He disguised his frailty to the end, finding his usual firm voice – though in a wheelchair – to record two days before he died.

Similar situations arose with the first two Dan Archers. Both Harry Oakes and Monty Crick were told: 'An understudy will take over until you are well again.' Sadly, in both cases we knew they would never recover and come back to us.

A happier story is that of Judy Bennett, who plays Shula. In the story Shula was sent to Australia for a fairly long visit. By the time she came back to Ambridge, her alter ego Judy had produced a baby girl, the proud father of whom was her husband Charles Collingwood (who plays Brian). Complicated, isn't it? Brian does get around, doesn't he?

I of course caused another absence (of Peggy) when we adopted David. The story was that Peggy had been ill with a throat infection to cover the change in voice when the new actress took over from me. In fact, Thelma Rogers' voice was so similar to mine that it all went smoothly.

Once David had settled in with us I came back as Rita Flynn until Thelma returned to the stage. There was confusion, at least in my mind, about my return. I had understood Thelma would be coming back after her season in rep and that I was standing in for her until she returned. As I was about to leave home for the studio my phone rang. It was a news reporter, who asked me how I felt about returning to my old part. I knew something wasn't right – a stand-in would not be publicised – so I said I had to leave immediately but that I would take his call when I got to Birmingham.

As soon as I arrived at the studio I went in to Tony Shryane. I told him the reporter seemed to think I was permanently back as Peggy. Tony said: 'You are.' Although it was good to be back, I felt terrible about Thelma, especially as I had already written to her, saying: 'Don't worry if you hear me as Peggy, I'm only standing in for you – it's your part.' I have felt bad about it ever since. Thelma and I worked together in other shows as well as *The Archers* and we had been friends. Sadly, we never met again.

With the return of Peggy it was decided the doubling of two major characters was not expected of an actor, even as they in effect got two characters for the price of one, so with regret I said goodbye to Rita Flynn. She married an old flame and went back to Ireland.

Characters' names and actors' names can become confusing to the public, especially in the case of married actresses. Opening a fête in the Cotswolds one day, Roger and I, plus David aged six, were entertained to lunch and my husband was seated next to the local vicar.

'It must be very confusing for you, Mr Spencer,' he said, 'having a wife called Mrs Archer,' to which Roger replied: 'Yes, especially when my name's Brocksom!'

After lunch a rather stately procession was organised with the local mayor and his lady, the vicar and various other dignitaries, together with me. We were solemnly and rather self-consciously making our way to the platform when David, waving a battered red fire engine, burst through the crowd. Rushing up to me, he shouted: 'Mummy, Mummy! Look what I found on the junk stall!' Everyone laughed, the atmosphere brightened and we continued on our way, feeling a lot more relaxed.

One actor who could never have done a 'double' was Jack May. He resolutely refused to change his very fine, distinctive voice to suit any character and so Nelson Gabriel, the village yokel and son of the old countryman Walter Gabriel, spoke in what can only be described as a 'posh' accent. Perhaps he learned to talk like that when he left the village to do his National Service in the RAF. Well, that's our story and we're sticking to it! Jack was always an amusing and well-liked member of the cast.

Over the years, there were times when we were in danger of being led in the wrong direction. Our editor (who had come from a less-believable serial than *The Archers*) once caused us to have a rather over-dramatic week when there was a plane crash, a quasi rape and even the church bells fell down! Stretching the listeners' credulity so far does us no good at all.

At other times things became so humdrum we were in danger of being taken off-air. Somehow we weathered the storms and for many years have gone from strength to strength. Times have changed, and we have changed with them. In 1973 a journalist wrote: 'So far the village has been spared abortion, homosexuality and drug addiction'.

Now, in the twenty-first century, we have treated all those sensitive situations but with sympathy and understanding, facing up to controversial subjects realistically and reaching out to listeners who find themselves forced to cope with similar problems. We give food for thought as well as entertainment.

There have been a number of character deaths over the years. It is, of course, an actor's fear. 'Am I going to be killed off?' is something at the back of any actor's mind during a drama serial and it often happens with undue warning. Anyone who has seen *The Killing of Sister George* will know what I mean.

To keep such a storyline from getting into the public domain is always a priority and we never throw away our scripts until after the due transmission date. The listeners do not like to know what is going to happen next – it spoils the illusion – but the press are only too anxious to get their 'scoop' and tell all.

Almost certainly the most famous 'death' in *The Archers* was that of Grace, which happened just by chance (or was it?) on the same night that commercial TV began. Chance or not, it stole all the publicity from everything else that evening.

The scripts for the episode of the fatal fire at the stables were kept under wraps until the very last moment – even the cast did not know beforehand, which was a nasty surprise for that popular actress Ysanne Churchman, who played Grace.

The nation was in shock and the BBC had to plead with the public not to send any more flowers. Norman was inundated with letters of condolence, many of them in genuine sorrow, obviously believing Norman – or Phil – was really a grieving widower. Years later, a group of us was enjoying a coffee break when Judy Parfitt (who played the district nurse, Janet Sheldon) arrived and cheerfully greeted us.

'You're looking very happy, under the circumstances,' someone said.

'*What* circumstances?' asked Judy.

'Well,' they continued, 'considering you've just been killed in a car crash. Didn't you know?'

'No,' said Judy, 'my scripts hadn't arrived before I left.'

Judy, of course, is a fine and busy actress so I suppose it wouldn't be quite such a blow to her as it might have been. We haven't had a district nurse since.

There have been a number of 'deaths' off-stage, too. Lilian Archer married twice and lost both husbands: first, Lester Nicholson (who died in Canada) and second, Ralph Bellamy (who died in the Channel Islands). Christine Archer married first Paul Johnson and afterwards, George Barford. Both husbands died. Jennifer Archer married Roger Travers-Macy and then divorced him. If I were an actor, I don't think I would want to risk marrying anyone called Archer! Of course Peggy married one, but as one of her grandchildren once remarked: 'Gran's a tough old bird!'

The only character to die with the consent of the actress was Doris Archer. Gwen Berryman's health was deteriorating and she had reached the stage where she felt unable to cope with travelling to the studio and the responsibility of carrying a central role so she resigned and entered a nursing home in Torquay. There she had two strokes and was crippled with arthritis. At the time of the broadcast of the death of Doris she was too ill to have listened. Several of us went down to visit her from time to time and take her out to lunch in her wheelchair. Sadly, we all went down again – this time for her funeral.

An unforeseen problem arose when Tom Forrest was accused of the manslaughter of a poacher. Tom was, of course, a gamekeeper. He was remanded in custody and then it was found that the courts were in recess so he would be out of the programme for some weeks. So how could Tom introduce the Omnibus with his usual topical chat if he was in prison? The illusion would be shattered – so Jack Archer had to step in and do the introduction instead.

Meanwhile, Bob Arnold (who lived in the Cotswolds) had problems keeping the illusion alive for more gullible listeners. He was once accosted in the street by an old lady who was an avid fan: she asked how he had managed to get out of prison. He told her that the prison had run out of fuel for the heating, so the Governor had let him go out for a time to get warm! She believed him and said it was kind of the Governor.

One must never take away the credit due to Godfrey Baseley for inventing *The Archers*. That said, he could be rather autocratic and I fell foul of him early on. He decided at rather short notice to hold a party for the cast and I regretfully said I couldn't go. I had already recorded *The Archers* that week and had made a second trip to Birmingham to do a radio play – three journeys up from Surrey would be too much in one week, I felt.

Denis Folwell (Jack) told me: 'I think you ought to go. Godfrey is very angry and is saying, "I'll have her out of *The Archers!*"' – we didn't call him God for nothing! 'How ridiculous!' I said, and stayed away. I think someone higher up thought the same so I'm still there.

In fact, Godfrey's abrupt manner caused a falling-out with the BBC and he wasn't there for the twenty-first year celebration at Broadcasting House. His contract was about to be terminated and he was too upset to join us. I felt this was sad, so I organised a luncheon party near to where he lived and a dozen of the long-standing members of the cast were there to greet him.

When he died, in 1995 the BBC organised a memorial evening in one of the big studios at Pebble Mill. Norman Painting talked about him and I read from Godfrey's favourite poem, 'The Everlasting Mercy' by John Masefield. He deserves to be remembered, especially as his brainchild *The Archers* is about to become an amazing 60 years old!

• Chapter 12 •

Pets and Other Creatures

Candy, our cat, did not approve of the arrival of David. If he cried, she would look at me accusingly and then retire to the airing cupboard. When he began to crawl and cornered her, she put him in his place with a smart pat on the hand, no claws. He got the message and thereafter respected her privacy.

For his third birthday we decided a hamster would be in order. Accordingly, we smuggled one hamster in cage into the house after he was in bed. We intended putting it by his bedside for him to find when he woke. In fact, it was we who awoke to see an ecstatic David by our bed, saying, 'I went into the lounge and there was a little mouse!' The 'little mouse' was in an open cage on the landing at the end of a long trail of sawdust. It was obviously a great success.

Ros, on the other hand, chose a budgerigar. I think she was hoping for a great talker, like my parents' budgie. He could give his name and address and laugh in exact imitation of my father's voice. Ros's budgie, always known to David as 'Lindy's stuffed budgie' – we called Ros 'Lindy' when she was little – was a fowl of another ilk. It never spoke and had a foul temper, no pun intended! Inevitably it fell to my lot to clean out the cage and when I let it out to do the cleaning I had to keep a perch in one hand to fend off its vicious attacks. Eventually, it was banished to my parents'.

Picnicking in the woods with the children one day we noticed a black mongrel that appeared to be on its own and when we went for a walk, it followed us. Someone in the car park told us he'd seen it several times: he thought it was dumped by some people in a van. The dog seemed to have attached itself to us and we hadn't the heart to leave it behind: it jumped willingly into the car and so we took it to our local police station. We told them that subject to Father's approval, we would adopt it.

'Well, it's all settled, isn't it?' said Roger, when he arrived home. So that's how Gyp came to live with us. He was a gentle dog with sad eyes but he was a wanderer. I once found him in the dog pound and brought him home but he went off again and that time we were unable to trace him.

David was disconsolate and so there was only one thing for it: a replacement. And that's how we acquired the bundle of mischief that was Pippin. He was a dog of mixed parentage, tremendous personality and intelligence. We bought him for the children and though they loved him and he shared in all their games, he was always known as 'Mother's dog'.

One day, against all the rules, they took him to a multi-storey car park that had just been built. He apparently jumped onto the wall round the top floor and fell, landing on the stout guy wire supporting a newly planted tree. That bounced him off onto the ground, grazed, but otherwise unhurt. A tearful phone call sent me rushing off to collect them – two very shamefaced children and an unrepentant dog.

Pippin was an escapologist of the first order. Going into

kennels at the vet's while we went on holiday was no contest as far as he was concerned. He soon found out how to open the door of his private quarters and was up and over the fence and trotting the mile to our house, where neighbours alerted my father who came and returned him to the kennels. The vet was mystified as to how he'd managed to scale an eight foot fence. It was wire mesh and he climbed it like a sailor, up the rigging.

If a bitch within miles was on heat he would be there – I could never settle for the night if he'd gone missing but in the small hours I would hear a very quiet, apologetic bark outside and he would come in, grinning and wagging from head to toe. One indignant lady found him in her kitchen with her very receptive bitch.

'How on earth did he get in? The door was closed . . .' she pondered. But the door handle was like the ones at home – he knew how to open those.

In desperation I asked the vet if he could give him something to make him less amorous. 'Well, you wouldn't want to spoil his fun, would you?' he replied. Then of course we couldn't!

Right from the start, Candy made it clear to him that she was boss and they got on well together, stopping to touch noses when they passed each other on the garden path.

When we built our new house in 1953 in Ashley Park, Walton-on-Thames, I had a kitchen large enough to accommodate my first washing machine. Actually, it was kept in a big cupboard and hauled out to the sink when needed. It was a twin-tub and had to be filled and emptied through a hose. David's imaginary friend lived in it – 'Hello, boy. You in dere?' he would say.

The room was what was known as a 'farmhouse kitchen' and was the hub of the house. A large breakfast nook took care of daytime meals and the kitchen was big enough to take a trestle table for tea when the children had parties. Candy had her basket on one worktop and although Pippin was also given his own comfortable bed, he preferred to sleep in the cupboard where we stored newspapers, flipping the door open with his paw.

He was very afraid of thunderstorms, as was my mother, so when we were woken by loud thunder one night I got up and went in to Mother, who was by then living with us. Suddenly I thought of Pippin and went downstairs to the kitchen. He wasn't in his basket or the cupboard – finally, I found him cowering right at the back of the cupboard under the sink so I took him upstairs to Mother's room until the storm passed.

If ever there was a storm in the night when I was a child I was woken up and taken downstairs. Mother would cover up any mirrors and make sure no cutlery was exposed – she thought they encouraged lightning strikes! Father would make a pot of tea and we all sat there until the storm was over. It is surprising that I too didn't grow up to be afraid of storms but in fact I revel in the drama. We get some cracking storms in Menorca. I wonder if the sea magnifies the sound for sometimes the noise literally makes you start up out of your chair.

Roger decided one day that he would put new paper on the kitchen ceiling. He found that he would need the help of a paperhanger's mate from time to time, so when he had pasted a length of it, he called me in from my gardening and I did what I came to call 'bat-upping'. For this I stood on a chair with the family cricket bat held horizontally over whichever end of the paper was draped. Somehow it worked.

Little Ros was always keen to join in David's games. I remember hearing her say to him: 'You bowl the ball and I'll crick it.'

When we moved into our new house we had half an acre of woodland. Over the years it evolved into a beautiful garden, with lawns, terraces, rock gardens and pergolas. Roger felled some of the trees but kept a small wood and he grew fruit and vegetables. I was in charge of the flowers. As I tugged up roots to make the first flowerbed suddenly they gave way and I fell backwards.

Immediately there was the sound of raucous laughter. It was my introduction to the beautiful green woodpecker (or yaffle).

We once found one lying dead in the garden and David insisted it should have a proper funeral. As we stood by the grave, he clasped his hands together and said: 'Please God, send another green woodpecker to live in our garden.'

As well as a wide variety of birds in the garden we had a lot of squirrels too. It was enchanting to see a whole family of baby squirrels running nose to tail through the trees, almost like running water. They did have their downside, though. One big grandfather of a squirrel repeatedly chewed his way through our caged rubbish sack until one day I said: 'Look, if I feed you, will you leave the rubbish sack alone?' He obviously knew what I meant – going into the larder to fetch him a crust, when I turned round I found he'd followed me into the kitchen.

Unfortunately he became a real problem for if I left the back door open, he was in and it reached the stage of me having to look through the window to check if he was about before I could open the door. When I met him in the hall one day I decided that was enough and stopped feeding him altogether.

An annual event was the parade of the baby mallards. There was a lake nearby where the mallards raised their ducklings and then the mother would lead them through the gardens: babies going under the fence, their mother over the top. When they reached the main road the traffic stopped while they crossed and then continued on through more gardens until they arrived at the Thames.

Occasionally a pair of mallards would visit us, marching up onto the terrace, where the female would settle down for a nap while the male watched over her. Then off they would go again.

The only thing that disturbed the peace of that garden was the Concorde flight path. I would rush out into the garden to see it go over, saying, 'You great big noisy, beautiful thing!' It never failed to move me.

I saw far more birds in our garden in Walton-on-Thames than I do these days in my country garden in Surrey. This may be partly because of the sad way in which many of the bird varieties are dwindling in number. In Walton, green and lesser-spotted woodpeckers were frequent visitors, as were tree-creepers, nuthatches, blackbirds and song and mistle thrushes. One mistle thrush was such a bully that I had to put bird feed at both ends of the terrace so there was always one free for the other birds to feed from.

Menorca has an even greater variety of birds. I have seen a purple heron there; also a kingfisher on the rocks by the house. Red kites, hoopoes, bee-eaters and charms of goldfinches were there in large numbers and many other rare varieties, if you knew where to look. Sadly, even there the numbers are dwindling though the shooting of wild birds is curtailed.

At home I never see a house sparrow although I know they are further down the lane. However, I have several varieties of tit and finches too now that I cater for their needs with niger and thistle seeds. The occasional visit of a woodpecker, nuthatch or a family of long-tailed tits is always a source of great pleasure.

This year a blue tit nested in the extractor outlet of my cooker so I couldn't use it for some time without blasting the family with hot air. Both parents worked non-stop throughout the daylight hours feeding their chicks – I just hope the magpies weren't waiting for them when they finally emerged as fledglings! Magpies have multiplied, unfortunately, and they decimate the eggs and young of other birds. There's nothing so cruel as nature.

I have a lovely memory of the days when Roger was alive, fit and well. In summertime he always preferred to take his afternoon tea indoors whereas I liked to have mine on my lounger under the damson tree in the garden. Promptly at four o'clock, he would appear with a little tea tray, which he would leave on the table beside me.

Immediately my tame robin would appear for his ration of crumbs. He would alight on the tray, once on the teapot lid and once on my knee. Both he and Roger are now gone – the damson tree too in the great storm of 1986.

Many years ago when I was young I watched a pack of dogs out on the spree. Their leader led them over a wall, leaving just one dog behind. Again and again, he tried to jump over the wall but in the end he just had to give up and go away.

That's what it's like to be old, I thought. And now I'm a bit like that old dog and I can't do half the things I used to do. I've had to realise that I can't walk far without getting tired; I can't dance anymore – or have more than one foot off the ground at any one time, either!

You can keep your age a secret until you're about 80 and then it's time to start bragging about it. You'll need to be about 65 before you can remember 'Have A Go' – a decidedly patronising radio quiz, compèred by the late Wilfred Pickles with wife 'Mabel at the Table', in which he asked simple questions of old-age pensioners and then asked: 'How old are you?'

'I'm 72,' might be the reply.

'Are you really?' Wilfred would say, 'Let's give her a clap!'

On ever-advancing birthdays now I look in the mirror and say: 'How old are you, luv?', 'I'm 90,' (or whatever) and then: 'Let's give her a clap!' and I fall about laughing.

My mother went to extraordinary lengths to keep her age a secret. She even scratched out the dates in her school prizes and wrote in later ones, which fooled nobody. You can only deny the years so far. It's sad, I think, to see the beautiful film stars of long ago, their faces distorted with nips and tucks, with tired old eyes and old hands – you can't disguise them.

These days I seem to drop things so much more often and it's such a long way down to pick them up – and even further getting up! But that is where the kindness of other people is so heart-warming. When I drop my stick, someone always picks it up before I can and hands it back to me with a smile. There are so many of us with sticks and it's rather like a brotherhood – we tend to smile at each other in passing. It seems there is a sort of unspoken pecking order: the young give way to the old – but not always – and the stick-wielders allow mothers with small children to go first.

Shop doors seem to get heavier by the year and some almost defeat me. That's when cunning kicks in: wait till someone else is going in and follow them close behind – then hope they're not someone who will let the door swing back in your face!

What I miss most of all, I think, is my inability to do more than a light potter in the garden. Time was when I entered my roses in the local horticultural shows – and even won sometimes. But I can still enjoy my garden with a little help.

In spite of man there is so much beauty in the world – flowers, music, sunsets, a young girl's lovely complexion and hair, a young man's handsomeness and strength . . . they are all food for the senses and soul. The view from my terrace in Menorca takes a bit of beating, too.

I was once asked what my ambition was for Peggy. Rather foolishly I replied that I would like her to be the first 100-year-old character in Ambridge before realising that if Peggy reached 100, I myself would be 107. Somehow I don't think I will be going to the studios then, though I have no doubt *The Archers* will be happily rolling on.

• Chapter 13 •
Name-dropping and Strange Requests

My work has brought me into contact with so many interesting actors: some already famous, others who went on to do great things. Of the former I was in awe of a rather strange-looking man due to him having lost an eye after being attacked by a dog. Esme Percy was a legendary figure and he and I, together with several other members of the cast, had dinner after the recording of *Bartholomew Fair*. Born in 1887, he was older than my parents. I was interested to find we had one thing in common: he had made his debut at the age of 17 in Nottingham with F.R. Benson's Company. Thirty years later, my own professional theatre debut in Nottingham was with the same company.

I worked many times with Howard Marion-Crawford, who later married Mary Wimbush. In fact, on the day of their first meeting 'Bony' (as he was known) and I were the leads in a radio play called *It Isn't Like Her* about an artist (Bony) and his sitter, (me) while Mary was making her radio debut in one of the smaller parts.

I met Denholm Elliott when we both auditioned for roles in a production of *Wuthering Heights*. He read with me for my audition and I read for his. The character I had to read for him was that of a child. Completely ignoring Denholm, the producer said to me, 'Oh, you can do child parts!' We both got the jobs – as brother and sister, though – and it led to a lot of work with overseas drama for me. At that time Denholm was a beautiful, dreamy young man and he spent any free time playing the piano in the studio.

One day in the early fifties a young man came up to me and said: 'You're June Spencer.' I agreed yes, I was and he told me: 'I'm Patrick Troughton.' I'm afraid I must have looked a bit blank because he added, 'Oh, you've never heard of me – but you will!' What a bighead, I thought. But he was right: he became one of the early Dr Whos and that's fame!

Two of the most charming people I met, although we never actually worked together, were Michael Denison and Dulcie Gray. At the time Dulcie was working at Pebble Mill on the BBC drama *Howards' Way* and we met by sharing a taxi from our hotel to the studio. Whenever she and Michael came to the Yvonne Arnaud theatre in Guildford, Roger and I would meet up with them for a drink after the show. As well as being a star of films, stage and TV, Dulcie is an accomplished authoress.

I first met John Arlott in a feature programme, not surprisingly about cricket, but he was taking part as a poet and reading one of his own poems. I worked with him many times later on when he was on the panel of BBC Radio's *Guilty Party*. After the recordings we all had some delightful lunches together and I was introduced to a few of the best restaurants in London.

I arrived at Waterloo after one very good meal and rang Roger to say, 'Don't wait lunch for me, I've had it.' To which he replied, with what seemed like a grin: 'Yes, I can tell!'

Only once in my life have I been legless and that was on holiday with Roger and friends in Menorca before we had our house there. We were in the habit of meeting in the bar before dinner to have just one champagne cocktail each. One evening we all thought that one ingredient had been left out – it seemed weaker than usual – so we had another.

During dinner I began to feel that if I didn't get up to our room at once I might not be able to make it later. So I rose to my feet, said, 'Excuse me' to the others then walked in a very straight line to the lift. On reaching our room I sat on the end of the bed without shutting the door and there I stayed until Roger arrived. Although my head was clear, my legs were completely useless.

'I'm so ashamed,' I told him. He grinned and said: 'It happens to the best of us' and then put me to bed. Next morning I apologised to our friends and told them what had happened. 'Oh, thank goodness,' they said, 'We thought we had offended you!'

Having learned my lesson the hard way, these days I content myself with a modest glass of red wine with my lunch – except when I am working!

When I was growing up my parents kept just a bottle of sherry for visitors in the house. I don't think they ever had wine at home and for them a special treat was to drive to a country pub, where Mother would have a cherry brandy and Dad would enjoy a glass of beer.

Roger and I were much the same and it wasn't until we bought our house in Menorca and the children were grown up that we began to have a glass of wine with our main meal of the day – 'Una dia sin vino es una dia sin sol' (a day without wine is a day without sun). Holidays were always different. At dinner dances in my youth escorts would buy me gin and lime – the thought of which is now obnoxious!

I've had some unusual requests over the years and one of the strangest, but most pleasurable, came out of the blue. In a nearby village stood a rather decrepit amateur theatre. It was well used and Roger and I frequently enjoyed their productions. Much as they loved their old theatre, the members had decided that it would have to go and they had come to an arrangement with the National Lottery to part-fund a new building themselves while the Lottery would subscribe the rest. Accordingly, a huge fund-raising programme was organised.

After a while I received a phone call from the very persuasive principal fundraiser: 'We shall be knocking down the old theatre and we thought it would be fun to have a "celebrity" in a hard hat on a bulldozer to strike the first blow. You know what I'm going to ask you?' 'I've always wanted to wear a hard hat and sit on a bulldozer!' was my reply.

In due course, I mounted my bulldozer in jeans and hardhat. I imagined they just wanted a photograph, but no – I was shown how to work the monster and soon I was bashing away, shouting: 'I've always wanted to bring the house down!' Eventually the splendid new Nomad Theatre rose from the wreckage and is a great asset to the neighbourhood – one gets invited to do the most unexpected things.

Another time I had a phone call from someone in a village in the Cotswolds. They were having a Battle of Britain commemoration week and part of the programme was a Brains Trust. Would I please consider being on the panel? I said: 'Are you sure you haven't got the wrong person?' They assured me it wasn't going to be too serious – they had a local poet and an Oxford student taking part. So I agreed to give it a go. When I told Roger he fell about laughing and then said: 'You haven't agreed, have you?' Not very flattering! In the event I did rather well and at least I made them laugh. The poet was charming but the student far too nervous to contribute much at all.

There have been so many celebratory lunches and dinners to mark the passing of the years that it is sometimes hard to remember which one was which. A delightful weekend was spent in Broadway in the Cotswolds celebrating one anniversary, another was held in the big studio at Pebble Mill, at which I was the speaker.

It came to be known as 'June's toy-boy speech' because at that time a lot of new young characters had been introduced into the programme and Peggy was being courted by a character who never actually spoke. I quipped that if ever he appeared, he might possibly be a toy-boy for her!

Among the hoards of celebrities present was Gillian Reynolds, who made the response in the form of an amusing poem. Gillian and I first met when we appeared in a TV programme about grannies and grandads (we were both the possessors of little grand-daughters).

I vividly recall another lunch at which Glenys Kinnock was the guest of honour – she is apparently a great fan of the programme. Her speech consisted of likening *Archers'* characters to her most-detested members of the then Conservative government. We listened in surprise and silence – and on my part in growing annoyance, particularly when she likened Chriss Gittins' Walter Gabriel to a personality who should have been killed off years ago. At that time he was very frail and I'm sure he could not but have been upset by her thoughtless remarks.

Succinct as ever in his reply, Jack May began with: 'Follow *that*!'

It seems all political parties have their *Archers'* fans. It was once my pleasure to meet John Major and his delightful wife Norma. Although he doesn't have much time to listen, she is a keen fan.

We met at St James's Palace when Prince Charles invited us for a huge get-together, together with the great and the good. It was both a privilege and a pleasure to meet and chat with Mrs Parker Bowles as she was then.

Paddy Greene and I had two very pleasant invitations together. As Jill and Peggy we were invited to visit a Norfolk village to open their new village hall. We stayed on a farm and enjoyed the hospitality of the local families.

We visited another farm, this time in Scotland, to present the cups at the local cattle show. On the way up on the train we joked about whether we should have to go up the garden path to the loo. We couldn't have been more wrong! Our host greeted us, driving an enormously luxurious car. Paddy whispered: 'We should have brought the little black!'

We found ourselves in the lap of luxury for the 'farm' was a huge country house. The hospitality we received from so many local people was amazing and we had a wonderful few days – our hosts couldn't have been more charming.

In the early days we were often invited to cattle and county shows. The Archers can still be seen there but these days they are not so suitable for an old lady such as Peggy!

For several years we took an 'Archers Addicts' stall at a big charity fundraising event at Loseley Park in Surrey. Several members of the cast stayed the weekend with Roger and me, others joined us the evening before for dinner. We manned the stall selling *Archers*' memorabilia and signing autographs for charity. They were very enjoyable, if exhausting weekends and one was rather painful – I was stung on my backside by a wasp!

On the occasion of a radio awards lunch at The Savoy hotel, Chriss Gittins and I were deputed to collect yet another award for *The Archers*. On arrival we were greeted by a young assistant who asked if we knew what we were there to do and I told her that we were there to collect an award on behalf of *The Archers*. She looked a bit startled and ran off. I didn't see her again, for at that moment luncheon was announced. Chriss and I were at different tables and after lunch came the awards.

One of the popular DJs of the day was acting as compère and he was badly briefed, to say the least. Eventually he announced: 'And now we have Jill Berrymor, who plays Peggy in *The Archers*, and Chriss Gittins, who is Walter Gabriel.' While I was trying to decipher that mixture of Jill Archer and Gwen Berryman (who incidentally was in hospital after a stroke) and identify it as meant to be me, my fellow guests were nudging me and saying, 'That's you.' Rather flustered, I joined Chriss on the platform.

The DJ went on to say, 'We also have Bob Arnold, who plays Tom', at which we shook our heads and said: 'No, we haven't.' By then we decided the only thing to do was to play for laughs, so I said, 'Sara Coward is here – she's Caroline.' Chriss cracked a joke and we were given an envelope to open. That was when it dawned on us that we were not there to be given an award but to present one to someone else.

I passed the envelope to Chriss, saying, 'You'll have to read this – I haven't got my glasses!' By this time he and I were leaning on each other and laughing – so too was the audience composed of all the big names in radio, including Vera Lynn and John Arlott, who had won an award and with whom we had been photographed in the Savoy garden.

Finally, the young assistant reappeared and presented each of us with a cheap little clock – which I gave to the next church bazaar. The bouquet of flowers, by way of apology from the BBC, was far more appreciated. Vera Lynn gave me a lovely smile in sympathy when I saw her afterwards in the foyer.

Another of *The Archers*' less successful ventures was a trip to Benidorm in conjunction with a travel firm to do the evening entertainment for an audience of elderly holidaymakers. We soon realised a specially written topical episode of *The Archers* was not what they were expecting; in a long, narrow venue with a crowd who would much rather have had a drink and a sing-song, we died the death.

How different from our experiences on the cruises. For our evenings of varied entertainment we have full houses of fans, enthusiastic and ready to join in.

Many years ago we were guests on a family quiz show on TV fronted by Bruce Forsyth. For technical reasons the recording suffered a long delay and I have tremendous admiration for the off-the-cuff way that Bruce went out and entertained the audience until we were able to get underway.

A fellow guest was the legendary Robertson Hare of the old Aldwych farces fame. I still remember his cry of 'Oh, calamity!' as he got the worst of every situation. Another big star of radio was Richard Murdoch of *Much Binding in the Marsh*. He joined us for one of the 'Simple Simon' Children's Hour pantomimes as did Terry Scott on another occasion.

The most star-studded cast I have ever worked with, however, has to be Graham Gauld's farewell production just before he retired. Graham started his career with the BBC, gaining experience as a studio manager doing sound effects with *The Archers*. As he has said, I was there on his very first day and then again in his final production, spanning his whole career.

The play was Noel Coward's *Waiting in the Wings*. Seasoned old trouper that I was, it was such a thrill to work beside Evelyn Laye, Mary Ellis, Dinah Sheridan (with whom I played my heart-rending scene) and Hannah Gordon. Other great names with whom I'd worked many times were Jill Balcon, Pat Hayes and Alan Wheatley. For once I asked everyone to sign my script and heading them all was Graham's 'For June – one of the first and best!' What a memory.

In the course of my work I have stayed in a great many hotels, most of them in Birmingham. These have varied from the grotty to the grand, from 19 shillings' bed and breakfast at the Grand Hotel in the distant past to the much dearer ones of today. Several of those hotels no longer exist – for example, The Queen's built over New Street Station caused one sleepless actor to phone down to the reception desk in the small hours: 'What time does this hotel get to Euston?'

I can remember some of us relaxing in the bar there after a live broadcast and particularly recall Marius Goring, who around then appeared in that marvellous film, *The Red Shoes*.

At the other end of the scale was a suburban hotel mostly

occupied by elderly permanent residents. The actor John Slater was also staying there and we agreed to breakfast together. The residents' conversation was conducted in hushed tones. Not so John and me. We chatted on, with John mentioning his wife, while I talked of Roger. Suddenly we realised all other conversation had ceased and icy stares were coming our way. They had obviously jumped to the conclusion that we were enjoying a dirty weekend – I don't think either of us stayed there again.

The most expensive hotels are not always the best, I've come to realise. In one such establishment, I found that I could only use the kettle sitting down. To switch it on while standing up, one's head was forced to be inside the lampshade of a suspended light fitting. On inspecting the bed, I could see no possible means of entry. Having moved four cushions and pillows, I was none the wiser. Finally, I realised the duvet was firmly tucked in all the way around, including the bed head – I can only think the chambermaid was a good deal stronger than me for it was a struggle to undo. The height of the bed was a further problem for someone of my stature: I could see the best way would be to take a running jump at it, but I'm past that sort of thing. Eventually, I managed to edge my way in, only to find the duvet came right over my head so I would probably suffocate. So, out of bed again: untuck the whole of the duvet and pull it down from the bottom. By this time the bed looked as if a tornado had hit it – some hotels try a bit too hard.

Just one other hotel memory before I move on – this time in Manchester. I had at that time a Suba Seal hot water bottle, which I left on the bed before going to the studio. Returning after a late broadcast, I found the chambermaid had considerately filled it for me and placed it in the bed. Unfortunately, she suba'ed it but had not sealed it, so I was confronted with a very wet bed.

Unlike my father, Roger was not a great one for sending

flowers on special occasions. When my parents' silver wedding was approaching, I asked Father: 'Are you going to send flowers to Mum?' To which he replied: 'I've already ordered 25 red roses.'

As I said, that wasn't Roger's scene though once in a burst of romanticism he greatly surprised me on holiday. Just before going down to dinner at the hotel in Menorca he presented me with a beautiful rose to wear. The next night, the same thing happened and so on, every night of the fortnight's holiday.

The morning before we left home he had cut 14 roses (from my rose bed!) and somehow packed them without me knowing. Once at the hotel he had them stored in the hotel fridge and collected one each evening. I was certainly impressed by his ingenuity and it was nice to know that I wasn't missing my roses by being away.

Chapter 14
The Awful Fortnight

When Father became frail my parents came to live with us and had their own private quarters. He had always been the staunch supporter of Mother and me, but he now wasn't able to give her the same help and I knew it was time for me to look after him. At 89 his health was failing fast.

Although virtually blind, he stubbornly refused to give up cosseting my mother and would pass me in the bedroom corridor without seeing me on his way to take a precariously balanced morning cup of tea to her room. Soon it became impossible and he was bedridden. Things got very difficult for he needed constant attention throughout the night and I was getting very little sleep.

My mother announced that as his wife she would look after him in the night, so we made a bed up for her in his room. The first night I heard him calling and eventually thought I had better go in to him. Mother had been asleep. 'I thought you were looking after him,' I said. 'Well, I've had my sleeping pill!' she told me. That arrangement was clearly not going to work so the next option was a short-term nurse until we could find a suitable nursing home for him.

The agency sent us a charming and gentle black nurse and Father took to him at once. Mother, on the other hand, barricaded herself in her room every night to our great amusement. In her sheltered life he was probably the first dark-skinned person she ever met. Goodness knows what terrors she imagined.

Father accepted his move to the nursing home with his usual good humour and the acceptance that he would probably never leave it. I took Mother to see him every afternoon except when I was away working. At that time I was still driving to and from Birmingham and on one occasion decided that I could drive home in time to see him before he settled in for the night and then return to Birmingham early the next day.

As soon as I'd finished recording (or so I thought), I was off but the next day when I walked into the studio I was greeted by Paddy Greene, who told me: 'You've an extra little scene to do – the one you missed last night.' They were all very understanding.

Father's perfect manners never deserted him. I took a neighbour in to see him one day. He said: 'I'm sorry I can't stand up but they won't let me get out of bed.' His favourite song was 'When I Grow Too Old To Dream'. Once, when I was there with Mother, he sang it all the way through, every note clear and perfect. When he had finished, he said: 'You didn't know I could still do that, did you?'

He was so delighted when David flew over from Germany to see him, but then suddenly he lapsed into a deep sleep. Roger and I cancelled our flight to Menorca to stay by him. The matron said he could remain in that state for a long time and advised us to take our holiday. 'You need it,' she told us and so we went after all. Roger's sister came to stay with Mother for the first week, Nora for the second.

Each day I phoned home and on the second day I received the sad news that a dear friend and neighbour had died. In the second week, when Nora answered the phone, she had to break it to me that my dear father had died too. We flew home immediately and Mother told me: 'I knew he had died before Nora told me – I heard him calling me in the night.' They had been married for 63 years.

I know that everyone thought my mother always imposed on me. When I was a child, Father once said to me: 'We wanted a little girl so that she could look after Mummy.' I remember feeling a bit disappointed. Was that the only reason why she had me, I wondered, but obviously I had taken it to heart. Although I loved my mother and I know she loved me, she was not always as supportive as my father and she could be queen of the put-down.

I also know she had the misfortune to have a rather jealous nature, maybe she resented my success just a little. Whatever I did for her, I did gladly. She had cosseted me in my early years and now it was my turn to look after her. Roger called her 'the fragile dictator' and didn't like her much whereas she thought the world of him and was very proud of her son-in-law.

I now come to a fortnight that I shall never forget, though not for any happy reason. Roger and I had planned to go to Menorca, but two days before we were due to fly I arrived home late from the studio to be told by my husband that he had been vomiting blood. I asked if he had seen the doctor and he said he hadn't in case he advised we couldn't go to Menorca! I told him we were not going anywhere while he was in that state.

After a disturbed night I rang the doctor very early on and Roger was rushed to hospital. Then I cancelled the flights and phoned our agent Francisco to tell him not to bring the car to the airport. Next, I called Ros, who at that time was working in Coventry, only to be told by her flatmate that she too had been taken to hospital that day with terrible back pain. Then my mother, now in a residential home, had to be told.

After a week Roger was allowed home with the necessary medication and I felt able to go up by train to Coventry to visit Ros in hospital. We had my mother to lunch on the Sunday, as we often did. Afterwards I took her to the local garden centre, where she enjoyed seeing all the beautiful flowering houseplants. I told her to choose one that she would like and she said: 'I'm not worth much.' 'Of course you are,' I told her and bought her a beautiful azalea. After that, I took her back to her room and we kissed and said goodbye.

That was the last time we were able to speak together. Two days later she had a massive stroke and without gaining consciousness, she died two days later – the day I was due to take her to have her hair done. Having been 'frail' for over 50 years, she finally died at the ripe old age of 94.

The following Monday I was back at the studio. 'Did you have a lovely time in Menorca?' they asked. 'No,' I replied flatly, 'we didn't get to Menorca. Roger was in hospital, Ros is still in another hospital and my mother died.'

In the meantime Ros had been discharged from the hospital and sent home wearing a steel corset which, they told her, she would have to wear for the rest of her life. This time I drove to Coventry and brought her back with me.

I took her to the wonderful osteopath who had cured me and it transpired she had exactly the same condition. She cured Ros as she had cured me and told her: 'You don't need to wear the corset – in fact, it was holding your pelvis in quite the wrong position.' In other words, it was doing her harm, not good.

Mother's attitude to life changed so much for the better during her stay in the home. She made friends with the charming old gentleman in the next room and he had obviously taken quite a shine to her. Mum had been woken one night by another old gentleman wandering into her room, which startled her more than somewhat, but her knight errant next door said: 'I've told her if he comes in again, she is to knock on the wall and I will come and rescue her. We can't have her frightened – she's such a dear little thing!' Not always as I would have described her. She could be quite the little troublemaker at times.

Elderly flirtations in old people's residential homes seem to occur fairly often. An aunt of mine carried things a bit far and was threatened with expulsion if she didn't simmer down a bit. Our bodies may age but that doesn't always apply to our libidos. Topical as ever, it looks as if a similar situation is developing in The Laurels, much to Peggy's consternation.

It's amazing how our attitude to old age changes as we ourselves age. When my father retired at 65, I felt my parents were ancient and needed to be looked after. Now I look at Father's retirement photograph all the while realising that I am now more than 25 years older than he was then. Mind you, the first thing he did when he retired and they came to live near us was to get a part-time job!

Age does strange things to our bodies. Everything is still there, just much lower down. So much of ageing is in the mind: if you think you're a poor old thing and life isn't worth living, it won't be. If you are lucky enough to enjoy good health, apart from all the inevitable drawbacks such as loss of hearing, a few aches and pains, etc., go out and make the most of what you've got left. Be an upbeat, not a downbeat! My mum used to say: 'Ah, the birds don't sing like they used to,' to which I would reply: 'They would if you'd wear your hearing aid.' We went through all the rigmarole of getting one for her but she never wore it.

• Chapter 15 •
Roger and Alzheimer's

When Roger's memory started to let him down, I soon began to fear he might be about to have the same problems as his mother. After my father-in-law died we had an increasing number of letters from Roger's mother that worried us. She complained that all her old friends had deserted her so we found a maisonette near to us and brought her to live where we could keep an eye on her.

We soon realised why her friends found it difficult to be with her as she was showing signs of dementia. I had frequent phone calls from the local post office where she had got into difficulties and it quickly became apparent she could no longer cope with living on her own. We moved her into a local nursing home, which by strange coincidence was previously the private school our children had attended.

One day she managed to walk out unobserved and tried to find her way to our house, half a mile away. She fell over and was picked up by a young man in a sports car. He kindly brought her the rest of the way so I was somewhat surprised when I opened the front door to them.

I made her a cup of tea while I phoned the residential home and after chatting for a bit, I drove her back. Alzheimer's patients are inclined to wander, so nursing homes tend to keep the outside doors locked. There was one old lady in the same home as my mother who always wanted to 'pop up to the stables for my mount'.

My mother had no memory problems – her greatest hazard was falling down a step because she was watching herself in the mirror at the same time! Mother-in-law herself had been a teacher and she seemed to think she was back with the children again and insisted on escorting the other old people to the lavatory. Eventually she died and now I could see some of those signs in Roger.

One by one, he fell out with his golf partners and finally gave up altogether. He would go into a sulk and eventually I would find out that it was about an imagined snub from someone. The repetitive questions were hardest to cope with. I soon took over the running of our affairs, although at first I always got his approval for any big decision. Then one day I told him about something, explaining in detail what I intended to do. Eventually he understood it, I felt, and so I breathed a sigh of relief.

A minute later, he said: 'Now wasn't there something you said we had to do about . . .'

'Roger, I've just told you!' I said.

'Well, tell me again,' he insisted.

It was all too much and he could see how upset I was but afterwards he seemed to accept he couldn't remember and the questions became fewer.

I had realised some time before that it was no good him going to see the doctor on his own. He'd had a persistent bad cough so

I made an appointment for him. When he got back, I asked him what the doctor had said.

'He gave me some stuff to put on that thing on my ear,' he told me.

'*What* thing on your ear? What about the cough?'

'I haven't got a cough,' he declared, rather indignantly.

After that we went together and he'd say to the doctor: 'June's going to do all the talking because I can't remember anything.'

For quite a while I was able to leave him to go to the studio. I would put together detailed instructions in very big writing (his sight was deteriorating) as to where I was, when I was returning and where he would find all his meals. One lunchtime he was entrusted to let a neighbour's dog out while she was out for the day, so I phoned him from my hotel as I always did to see how he was getting on.

'I let Di's dog out,' he told me.

'That was tomorrow you were supposed to do it,' I said, but I couldn't help wondering if she had been in the house when he did it. Even Alzheimer's has its funny side – though not often.

Roger used to enjoy a gin and tonic but when his memory began to fail he was apt to forget if he'd had a drink and pour another. I had to keep an unobtrusive eye on him so that he didn't have more than was wise! He didn't want to go out or do anything unless it was with me: I could see how some sufferers become recluses and cease to look after themselves. Now Roger's only memories were of his wartime service in Burma – we had no shared memories anymore.

Then one day he had a series of TIAs (Transient Ischaemic Attacks) and I took him to hospital. It was decided to keep him in over the weekend and all being well, I could bring him home on the Monday afternoon. When I visited, the other men on his ward said he kept them awake talking in the night and seemed to be under the impression he was on a ship going to India. I knew, of course, that he had been reliving his war experiences again.

On the Monday I returned from shopping in good time to go and collect him from the hospital. I was surprised to find a taxi on the drive and Roger wandering about in the rain. He had apparently become tired of waiting for me and had walked out, got in a taxi and arrived home. No money, no door key, no belongings and no discharge papers from the hospital! Ros arrived in time to go to the hospital and sort it all out. He simply could not cope with strange environments.

When we were on holiday in Menorca in November 2000 he had a stroke and with the help of our friends, Bob and Josie, an ambulance was called and he was taken to hospital. Although I stayed with him in his room night and day, he was completely lost. It was as if he was in the last stages of Alzheimer's, raving and trying to get out of bed. There was a pullout bed for me but I got virtually no sleep and after a few days, I was totally exhausted.

That was when my good friend Francisco came to my rescue. It is he who manages my affairs in Menorca and he had visited Roger every day. He could see the state I was in and he told me: 'Go home, get some sleep – I will stay with him until midnight, and come again at six in the morning and wait until you come.' What a friend.

After that I sent out an SOS to Ros – who, bless her, dropped everything and flew out to help me. Once Roger was discharged, he reverted to his usual state. I feel sure he must have been given some sort of medication that had confused him so much.

We brought him back to England in a wheelchair. Alzheimer's can affect people in different ways. Roger never became aggressive and he was always gentle and co-operative with me, though he could sometimes upset other people with an abrupt, rude attitude. As I have already mentioned, quite early on he had fallen out with his golfing friends and gave up playing. He then became totally reliant on me.

'How did I get like this?' he once asked, while recovering from the stroke. I told him that he had had a stroke.

'Was it here?' he continued.

'No, in Menorca,' I told him.

'Tell me about it,' he said.

So, I told him about the stay in hospital, how I had stayed with him in his room and Ros had flown out to help get him home.

'I don't remember any of it,' he said, 'but it must have been awful for you.' Typically, no self-pity – just thought for me.

Life became very difficult for Roger. He had been an avid reader but now his sight was deteriorating and though I got large print books for him, he would say 'This book's rubbish' – I knew it was because he was unable to remember what had gone on in the previous paragraph. The same applied to TV plays and there were few programmes he could enjoy sitting close to the set.

After pushing him round the house in a wheelchair for some time I got a walking frame to get him back on his feet again. I think he was quite content not to bother doing anything for himself and when I was out one day and Ros was sitting with him she was rather amused when he said in a slightly puzzled voice: 'Does your mother want me to walk again?' Naturally, Ros replied: 'Yes.'

For me to cope on my own with someone who couldn't remember anything from one moment to the next, who didn't want to do anything for himself was getting a bit much. Also, it wasn't doing him any good. He found that he was quite capable of walking with aid and soon graduated to sticks so I organised visits from a physio.

I would say: 'Lucy comes today.'

'Who's Lucy?'

'She's the girl who has you on the bed, every Tuesday morning!'

We have a very good neighbour who Roger liked and he sometimes took him out, which gave me the chance to do the hoovering – a noise Roger didn't like.

I took him shopping with me and he stayed in the car, watching the comings and goings. When I finished, I'd say: 'Now we'll go home and have a nice cup of coffee.' And he always replied: 'That sounds *lovely!*'

He remained good-natured and uncomplaining, and we still took pleasure in each other's company. After six months he had learned to walk again with the aid of a stick.

One beautiful day during May 2001, two days before our fifty-ninth wedding anniversary, I said: 'It's such a lovely day, let's have lunch in the garden.' I helped him out and sat him under the sun umbrella. We sat amid the spring flowers and enjoyed a nice salad and a bottle of chilled white wine. He kept on saying: 'Isn't this lovely? What a lovely lunch!'

It is a treasured memory for less than 24 hours later, without warning he died. Tragic as it was, we were at least spared the last awful stages of Alzheimer's.

Some time afterwards I went out to Menorca on my own. As I sat dozing in the living room on that first afternoon suddenly I became convinced Roger was sitting opposite. I was so certain that when I opened my eyes and he wasn't there, I could scarcely believe it.

I thought no more of it until I got up the next morning. On my way to open the shutters, I smelled smoke. Immediately I stopped but before I could search for the source, the smell vanished. I walked on and suddenly there it was again. Then I realised that what I could smell was tobacco smoke (Roger had been an avid pipe-smoker). So then I knew: how lovely – he had come with me!

In 2004 there was an extraordinary coincidence. I was again staying alone in Casa Ruisenor and when turning, caught my foot on a chair leg and fell heavily to one side. Those tiled floors are hard and I knew I was in trouble. As I lay there, I said out loud: 'You stupid old woman – you've broken your hip!'

I knew there was no one near by so it was no use calling for help but by the grace of God I had fallen by a low table and on it was my mobile. A call to Francisco and he was there within minutes and called an ambulance. It was not my hip – I'd broken my femur and was taken to the same hospital on the same day, 7 November, to which Roger had been taken, exactly four years before.

Again, Francisco proved his friendship and again, my wonderful daughter and her partner flew out to help me and eventually got me home, where David nursed me so tenderly until I was back on my feet again.

It wasn't the first time I'd had an incapacitating fall, though. Back in 1949 I was working for Edward Livesey on a programme that was to be transmitted live at 11pm that night. While crossing the road I fell on the base of my spine and was in considerable agony. Philip Garston-Jones, who at that time was a producer of thriller serials, came out of his office, picked me up and carried me up two flights of stairs to the BBC club where he bought me a brandy.

Until we went on air I spent the rest of the time lying on my stomach on a couch. After that, I had years of pain before being cured by a wonderful osteopath. The listeners have no idea under what conditions we sometimes have to work!

Many was the time I worked for Philip and I particularly remember one six-part serial called *Red for Danger*, in which I played a woman called Red. After the final episode the cast were entertained to dinner by a local business consortium and as the leading actress I was delegated to give the vote of thanks to our hosts after dinner.

I rose to my feet, said a few well-chosen words, sat down . . . and disappeared under the table! Our host had considerately pulled my chair back as I stood up, but neglected to put it back again.

The question most asked by the listeners is: 'Do you have to learn the lines?' 'No, thank goodness!' is the answer to that. We receive the scripts several days in advance so that we can work on them before we get to the studio. Following this, we sit round, read the whole script and then go into the studio, scene by scene. That is when we rehearse with sound effects before we record. One episode takes about two hours and 15 minutes to record.

I am sometimes asked if I'm like Peggy. We both love cats and enjoy our gardens but Peggy rarely displays a sense of humour while mine shows at unsuitable moments. Of course, we have one thing in common at present: both Peggy and I have been carers of a husband with Alzheimer's.

When our editor Vanessa Whitburn decided to do a storyline on Alzheimer's and chose Jack Woolley as the most likely candidate, she very considerately asked me how I would feel about acting a role I had experienced in real life. I immediately supported the idea as an ideal way of bringing awareness of this dreadful illness before the public and portraying the stressfulness of being a carer. Roger had constantly given me such support all the years of my career. Once when I was feeling depressed about the way things were going and was thinking of giving up, he said: 'Don't – you know you'd miss it if you did.' How right he always was.

I was invited to the next script conference where I was asked to talk about my experience of caring for Roger and how I had first noticed all was not well with him. A highly sympathetic assembly of writers and directors asked searching questions. Much of what I told them that day was mirrored in future scripts, which have been throughout so beautifully and sensitively written. There is, of course, a doctor who keeps a watching brief over all medical storylines too.

In the early scenes of Jack's Alzheimer's the parallels between his symptoms and Roger's were identical. When Peggy took Jack to see the specialist and he was given the Alzheimer's tests it was like reliving my past. I too took my husband to consult a specialist and watched as he failed the same tests, one by one.

There was a very poignant moment as Roger and I sat in the waiting room waiting to see the specialist. We sat quietly and after a few minutes Roger leaned over to me and whispered, 'You're not going to leave me here, are you?' I felt like crying, but I told him cheerfully: 'Of course not – you're coming home with me.' But it gave me an insight into the fear and insecurity he had and I realised that I no longer had a strong man who would look after me but someone as vulnerable as a little child who looked to me for protection.

I had had a similar feeling towards the end of my father's life. He who had been a rock all my life now resembled my child in his frailty and dependency. In both cases it brought such an upsurge of love and compassion.

In the programme I sometimes felt I was sitting next to Roger instead of Jack as we recorded scene after scene of poignant incidents. Soon fact and fiction diverged as Jack became unreasonable and then violent. Although Roger was never violent, the stress of coping with Jack's demands causes exhaustion in Peggy as a carer and that was something I could relate to.

I had been able to keep my head above water and I kept going through being highly organised and calling on my sense of humour. Peggy's ordeal was so much harder – Jack saw to it that she rarely had a decent night's sleep and that is a killer.

I did have some experience of that when Roger was in hospital in Menorca after the stroke. In that strange environment, surrounded by people who spoke an unfamiliar language, he became like Jack in the later stages of Alzheimer's. He tossed and turned, raving all night, so that I had no sleep and was soon a mental and physical wreck, as Peggy later became. Once I came back after a brief trip to buy food and found to my horror that he had been restrained – his hands and feet were tied to the bed. The whole experience gave me insight to portray Peggy's plight.

I dreaded the day when Roger wouldn't know who I was and I would have to let him go into a nursing home. For us that day never came, thank God, but I knew just how Peggy must have felt when she had to let Jack go.

The Alzheimer's story opened up new avenues. Already I had volunteered as a guinea pig in tests for the disease and I was then approached by the Alzheimer's Research Trust and asked if I would give a talk about being a carer, both in *The Archers* and in real life. My speech was to be at The Royal Society, no less! Fortunately it was well received and resulted in a big press coverage, which gave good publicity not only to the Alzheimer's Research Trust but also to the programme and resulted in my being asked to become a Patron of the Trust.

We have since added to *The Archers'* many awards by winning a Mental Health BAFTA in 2007 for Jack and Peggy's Alzheimer's story. Arnold Peters and I were so warmed by the reception we received when we went up to collect it.

• Chapter 16 •
What is Acting?

What is acting, and why do I love it so? Most children play at 'Let's Pretend' – I know I did from an early age. As we grow older reality steps in, but for some that game lingers on and I suppose we are the ones who embark on the precarious profession of being an actor.

To me it is endlessly fascinating to temporarily assume someone else's life, with all their feelings and emotions. I have 'been' Mary, Queen of Scots having a heated argument with John Knox. I played Lady Jane Grey in conversation with the Archbishop of Canterbury shortly before her execution (without going under the axe, thank goodness!). In the case of my long-standing alter ago Peggy, I slip her on like a familiar old coat when I go into the studio, suffer her woes and then slip her off and become myself again when I come out. I think I would know by now how she would react in any given situation, even if my own reaction might be quite different.

It was a great compliment early this year to be invited to be the castaway on Radio 4's *Desert Island Discs*, a programme I have loved since its earliest days when I first went to London to live. With *ITMA*, *Tuesday Serenade* and *The Man in Black*, it was my favourite source of entertainment.

I have always enjoyed music and to be allowed to choose discs to be played especially for me was rather like being a child let loose in a sweet shop. However, I soon discovered it was no easy task to curb my enthusiasm and confine myself to just eight discs. Not my favourite eight pieces of music, either, but eight that had special associations for me.

My tastes are not highbrow – I like a good tune but there wasn't space for the piano and violin concertos that I love, and I would have liked to have been able to fit in more opera and some Beatles' numbers – I love to hear Plácido Domingo sing 'Yesterday'. To my mind he is the only operatic star who can sing popular tunes without sounding pretentious.

I was interviewed at home to discuss various aspects of my long life and to say which discs I would like. It was such a pleasure to meet Kirsty Young. What a great interviewer she is. Immediately I was at ease and felt I could chat with her as if we were old friends.

I was absolutely astounded at the reaction to the programme and the many letters I received from listeners who could identify with me and shared our mutual problems. What pleased me most were the generous compliments of my fellow actors. What wonderful friends they all are. It was intriguing to eavesdrop on the comments online. They say eavesdroppers never hear good of themselves – well, it seems to have been mixed!

Message: Having seen her photo in today's *Daily Mail* it struck me that she looks like I imagined Jill to look. How confusing is that. I don't look at actors' photos because Ambridge exists totally in my mind. Yes, I know that is sad.

Message: I always knew that Peggy wasn't real. I have never thought of booking a room at Grey Gables (like people apparently did for Crossroads Motel) but somehow I feel so ashamed for my deep-seated hatred of Peggy, having just heard June Spencer on *Desert Island Discs*. How nice she is. My confusion is now total.

(**Me:** I did say they were mixed reactions!)

Message: Amazing how – to me – she sounds younger than Peggy! Peggy has an almost tremulous way of speaking, making her sound frailer compared to June.

(**Me:** You'd sound frail, too if you'd been through what Peggy has! It's called 'acting'.)

Message: It was interesting. I was particularly struck that both the actor and prod team think that Jack is portrayed as aggressive. What I hear is someone who is quite biddable. I've experienced aggressive behaviour and it's nothing like Jack and would make very upsetting listening if they attempted to portray it.

(**Me:** Didn't they hear the episode when Jack physically attacked Lilian?)

Message: Just listening to Peggy, aka June Spencer on *DID*. Really good – I'll have more patience with Peggy now that I know something more about her character. June is in her nineties, which I didn't know, and she nursed her own husband with Alzheimer's. Lovely nostalgic music she chose too. Reminded me of *Family Favourites* on Sunday lunchtimes in the 50s and 60s.

Message: June is a fine, strong-hearted actress. Her own experience might not be exactly the same as Peggy's but it brings such power to the storyline. I'm glad she has a happy memory of her real-life husband before he changed and her son, too. Wonderful listening.

(**Me:** You see, not everyone hates Peggy!)

Message: I was really surprised that 'Barwick Green' wasn't one of her musical choices.

Message: I have 'Barwick Green' on my ring-tone on my phone.

Message: Me, too

(**Me:** And you have no idea how many other people – some very famous – do too!)

Message: I seem to remember when I were a little lass listening to *The Archers* that Peggy, married to Jack Archer and running The Bull, was somewhat common – not the wise, posh-sounding matriarch of today? Or has my memory let me down over 50-odd years?

(And that is when I came out of my eavesdropping mode.)

The above message makes a valid point: Peggy had a slight cockney accent in the early days. She was the townie character, the one who knew nothing about life in the country. As country ways were explained to her, the programme also educated townie listeners.

When Jack Archer died and Peggy went to manage Grey Gables I felt she would make a conscious effort to speak like the wealthy clients. An intelligent woman, she realised that her way of speaking did not match the importance of her job.

One has to be very wary of dialects on air – too strong a dialect can result in the character becoming unintelligible to the listener. In broadcasting to schools we had to adopt a slower, very distinct way of speech to be clear to a class of children with perhaps an old-style radio.

There are so many different facets to radio acting, one never stops learning – and of course broadcasting equipment has changed over the years. The new digital microphones are so sensitive they pick up the slightest sound, especially the unintentional rustle of one's script. We have to do more retakes for that than anything else. Beware too the late-morning recording – a tummy rumble wanting its lunch can be deafening.

To go from theatre to radio acting is a whole new ball game. There is no feedback from a live audience and therefore the timing is different. Scenery must be transmitted to the listener through voice and sound effects. In *The Archers* the sound effects are so numerous that every outdoor scene has a background of authentic sounds: traffic, tractors, farm animals and bird song. And the right birds singing the right song for any particular time of year must be exactly right – there are hundreds of bird-watching enthusiasts who will let us know if we get it wrong.

What are known as 'spot effects' are done in the studio: doors, windows opening, crockery, the filling and boiling of kettles and newspaper rustling (as opposed to scripts!) all done by the studio manager.

Telephone conversations when both ends are heard are done by the distant one sitting in a separate little studio wearing headphones and go ahead just like a real phone call. In addition to the 'telephone kiosk', the main studio is divided into five areas, all acoustically different.

A big open space is for village halls, large rooms at Grey Gables, the church, etc. – anywhere there might be a slight echo. There is a smallish enclosed area with chairs and a settee (which doubles as a bed), where a cosy room would have no echo such as a sitting room or bedroom. Another area, somewhat less enclosed, is where kitchen scenes, the interior of The Bull or the village shop are recorded. This contains a kitchen sink, Aga, fridge and cupboards plus a table and chairs. Just outside that is used for hallway scenes.

The final area is known as the 'dead' studio with special walls so there is no possible echo. This is used for outdoor scenes. If we need to denote walking, gravel is spread on the floor – or straw as the case may be. In the main area is also a staircase (that doesn't lead anywhere!). It is partly carpeted so that it can be used either way.

When recording is about to start, a red light appears on the wall followed by a green light for the scene to begin. More than once I've overheard someone say: 'I don't listen to *The Archers* because I can't stand so and so and the way he or she does this and that!' Clearly, they most certainly *do* listen.

Before we begin rehearsing at the microphone we have a 'read-through' and this is where we are sometimes taken unawares by a double entendre in the script. The actors have a good laugh and get it out of their systems. One gem turned up in a schools' broadcast about the universe. Charles Stidwill had great difficulty in keeping a smile out of his voice while saying, '. . . and if you hear a strange noise you will know I have just passed an asteroid!'

Some of the early Children's Hour plays and serials in which I would play little girls were written by elderly ladies; in one I had to exclaim, 'Golly gumsticks!' How silly, I thought, no one would ever say that – but I was wrong. Quite recently I was handing in a bag of jumble at the village hall. The elderly lady on the receiving end said: 'Oh dear, more! Golly gumsticks!'

One of those elderly authors visited the studio for the final episode and invited the cast out to tea at a nearby hotel. I think she was possibly taken aback to find no children, just grown-ups, and thought that tea was perhaps not quite suitable so she came round to each of us in turn with a flask, asking if we'd like a little brandy in our tea!

Over the years we have held a number of conventions and it is always so good to meet our listeners, many of whom look upon us as old friends. Most have been held in the country environment where activities such as welly whanging (a competition to see who can throw a Wellington boot the furthest) may be held. This once led me to make a rather embarrassing faux pas. I was intending to tell someone where to find the welly whanging but unfortunately it came out as the 'willy wagging'. Oh dear!

The biggest-ever convention was held in the Birmingham Exhibition Centre on 8 September 2001. We filled the huge arena with stalls and events but the crowds were so great that we found it difficult to move around to get to the various stands where we were supposed to be.

An optional dinner hosted by 'Jack and Peggy' was well patronised. In the evening we were all on stage being interviewed, two by two, by the late Nick Clarke. We even had two 'dead' members of the cast there: Young John Archer (who died under a tractor) and Phil's late lamented wife Grace. As 'Jill' remarked rather tartly: 'Doesn't nearly 50 years of marriage and four children count for anything?' The audience loved that.

The illusion that characters in *The Archers* are real people overheard rather than actors is still kept up in that a cast list is never read on air unlike all other radio drama. If anyone wants to know who plays a particular character they have to look in the *Radio Times*, which publishes a cast list once a week. Hence, although my name was fairly well known to listeners many years ago because of the numerous productions in which I acted, new generations have grown up and while 'Peggy' is well known, 'June' would not be so familiar to many people.

After my appearance on *Desert Island Discs* I had a letter from an 88-year-old gentleman, who began: 'June Spencer, Desert Island Discs. Never heard of you.' But he went on to say how much he had enjoyed the programme and that it had greatly heartened him. In reply I told him that I had never heard of him either but I was delighted he had enjoyed it. Such letters are a joy to receive.

Generally, we radio actors have a fair degree of anonymity but so often our voices can give us away. I once shared a table on a river cruise with five very pleasant people. The first evening we were introducing ourselves to each other. One couple were both schoolteachers and an older couple were retired schoolteachers – I allowed them to think I was just an elderly widow. The second evening at dinner the elder man began asking me questions, very politely trying to find out what my work had been. It was rather like the game of Twenty Questions. Finally, he cornered me and I had to come clean and say that I was an actress in *The Archers*. The lady sitting next to me said: 'We'd sussed you out last night.'

It pays to be careful what you say in public places. I have been overheard, recognised and approached by someone from a nearby table for an autograph. On one occasion I was asked to sign a paper napkin for a 'friend who is a great fan'. A year later I saw the same person again and was told the recipient was so thrilled that he had framed it!

Occasionally we are recognised, sometimes in the most unexpected places. Dining with Roger in a restaurant in Florence I couldn't help but notice a man from a distant table always appeared to be staring at me. Eventually he came over and asked if I was an actress. When I admitted I was, he said: 'My wife is in *Waggoners' Walk*.' I was so surprised that I never thought to ask her name.

Maybe my appearance on two recent *Songs of Praise* programmes is making me more recognisable. At an airport a woman smiled at me and asked: 'Should I know you?' My companion said: 'Yes!' The woman then said: 'I'm a keen Archers Addict.'

There are no stars in *The Archers*. It is something that has been understood by the cast since the very beginning and only rarely does it cause a problem. Invariably, young and talented members of the cast leave to pursue wider careers and we are always proud and happy for them when they do well. Some manage to combine theatre and TV work with their appearance in *The Archers* – notably Tamsin Greig, who has become an award-winning star of stage and TV but remains faithful to us and returns to Ambridge from time to time to visit her 'family' and confer with Brian over their farming partnership. No 'star' complex there!

I can think of only one person who has broken the mould. Although a very good actress and popular with the public, behind the scenes she just didn't fit in: she was always criticising the performance of her fellow actors and generally behaved like a prima donna, expecting special privileges. To the relief of us all, she finally flounced off. Phew! We don't do 'sensational' in *The Archers*.

Sensation in the programme is quite another thing. Every so often Ambridge is shaken up by a scandal, such as Jennifer's baby. More recently we have had a rape storyline. It happens in real life and it is right that we should illustrate the trauma and the dreadful effect it has on the victim and her family. Such an episode is dealt with sensitively rather than with sensationalism.

The tale of Brian's affair and the resulting baby grabbed the nation's attention. Over the years, it has been hinted that Brian was not adverse to a flirtation here and there but this time the listeners were practically in bed with them! Brian was genuinely in love with both women: his wife Jennifer and mistress Siobhán. It was tragedy for him in Siobhán's death, tragedy for Jennifer and his daughter Alice, who found it so hard to come to terms with what her father had done – and it certainly aroused the rage of Peggy, his mother-in-law, who wanted to horsewhip him (I enjoyed playing that scene).

It was compassion all round for the little boy Ruari, which helped to heal the wounds. Ruari was played by a child who lived in Ireland – his brogue had to be authentic so one of the directors travelled to Ireland to record his lines, which were then fed into the scenes as they were rehearsed and recorded. We actors could hear his voice and talk back to him but we never actually met him. We all wanted to – he sounds such a delightful chap.

That is the case with all the very young children that you hear in the programme. In the early days some of us doubled the children's speeches. I played the young Jennifer, while Ysanne Churchman was Lilian. Judy Bennett is also a brilliant child impersonator.

Nowadays, you always hear the genuine article, though.

Usually there is a gap of a few years and then you will hear them again as schoolboys or girls, often played by 12- or 13-year-olds. They have to be accompanied to the studio by a parent or guardian, who stay with them all the time. We do everything by the book. Sometimes they stay on, ageing with the character as they grow up. There are some actors who came to us as teenagers long ago, who now have children of their own – and in some cases, grandchildren. We are a real-life dynasty as well as a fictional one.

With such a huge cast almost no one can make a living by appearing solely in *The Archers*. In the early days of a small cast we would be on either a six-month or ongoing contract. Nowadays we are employed by the episode so work can be very spasmodic, according to the storyline.

The cast is continually evolving. Many actors will appear for just one storyline, but the regular characters, though working intermittently, develop and age in real time.

It is amazing to think that when *The Archers* began George VI was on the throne. Everywhere we went we had to carry our identity cards and now many people here have been up in arms because of the recent talk about bringing them back again. Sweet rationing didn't end until 1953 – probably having unlimited sweets again didn't do our teeth any good at all. Until 1954 some food was still rationed and we all had ration books that we had to surrender whenever we shopped for the coupons to be cancelled. Cars were still comparatively thin on the roads and the first section of the first motorway, the M1, opened in 1961.

If I count Edward VIII who succeeded but was never crowned, I have lived through four reigns. Even more amazingly, my parents survived six reigns, having been born during the reign of Queen Victoria.

Little did I think in 1950 when I took on the role of the 26-year-old mother-of-two that today I would still be playing that same character, albeit 84 and a grandmother of seven plus one, deceased. The last one 'died' to allow him to pursue his career elsewhere and I mustn't forget Kate made Peggy a great-grandmother.

From time to time certain eminent people have described us as a 'national institution' and that gives us all a certain responsibility. Over the years we have become a programme of integrity and we are proud of that. That is not to say that we are smug – we all know one of the secrets of our success and survival is the down-to-earth nature of the programme, no pun intended! So far we have not let the public down with any unsavoury scandals among the cast. We're a bunch of diverse human beings who care about – and support – each other and we enjoy the pleasures of this life as much as anyone else.

Births and marriages among the cast are greeted with the joy of any 'family' and I can personally vouch for the way both cast and production staff helped celebrate my milestone birthdays. In turn, the love and support I was given on the death of my husband and son touched me greatly – *The Archers* is indeed my second family.

Although I am by nature a rather private person I have not hesitated to talk openly and publicly about two subjects close to my heart. When we began the Alzheimer's story it was an illness that was not talked about very much – a relative with dementia was not something to tell everyone about. The situation is very different now and I think we played a small part in changing public opinion. Brought out into the open it helps to create understanding, sympathy and help – and hopefully in time a fair share of money towards finding a cure for this dreadful disease that gradually takes away the minds of the most intelligent and intellectual people.

My husband had Alzheimer's. It is not something you die of and he succumbed to a stroke while he still knew me but I saw enough to know what it could do to a once lively and supportive man. I had experience too of what it is like to be a carer. The

Alzheimer's Research Trust has my fervent support in their quest to find a cure and also the work done by the Alzheimer's Society.

Chapter 17

David

When the children were old enough we followed the traditional pattern and sent Ros for dancing classes and David to the stables for riding lessons. It soon became apparent that neither was suited – so we swapped them.

Ros adored riding, while David at once showed an aptitude for dancing. When he was seven, he confided in me: 'I can't make up my mind whether to be a great ballet dancer – or have a garage.' Dancing won and when he was 11, he was accepted at the Rambert School of Ballet.

He was 17 and a student there when he was offered a contract to join the State Ballet Company in Kiel, Germany. We knew this was where his future lay – there was so much more work for classical dancers in Germany than in England. Every state has a subsidised theatre for productions of opera, ballet, musical comedies and drama: once in the system dancers can move from one state to another, almost like being in the Civil Service.

Because David was under 18 we had to appear before a judge in his chambers to seek approval and then our son would be placed in the charge of the British Consul in that part of Germany. The judge told us that usually it was for the safety of young girl dancers but in David's case, he said with a twinkle, it was more likely the German girls would need protection!

We all went to Heathrow to see him off. As we were able to see his plane, we waved in the hope that he might see us up on the observation deck. I was fine until I noticed a sparrow feeding its baby and then it hit me that my fledgling was leaving the nest so my family led me away in tears.

Thereafter, David danced in Kiel, Kassel, Wiesbaden, Munich and Augsburg, ending up as second principle soloist in Braunschweig. He was a wonderful partner in pas de deux with his then wife; also a brilliant character dancer. As Dr Coppelius in *Coppelia* he brought out the pathos of the old inventor as well as the comedy and obviously captured audiences, as we ourselves witnessed. When David took his solo curtain call on the night when we were in the audience Roger asked: 'What's that noise?' 'They're stamping for him,' I replied. Even now the memory of it brings tears to my eyes. We were so proud of our son.

Roger, Ros and I saw every production he was in on our many visits to the various parts of Germany. On one occasion I was due to record *The Archers* on Monday so I left Kiel on the Saturday to fly from Hamburg and be home in good time. There was a delay, we were told, because England was closed down by fog. Eventually we were all put into a hotel for the night but the next day – Sunday – the situation was the same. I was beginning to panic about not being back in the studio on time.

Then I overheard someone say they could go by train to the Hook of Holland and cross by boat, so I decided to do the same. I had just enough money for the fare, got my ticket, reclaimed my luggage and somehow found the train. That night on the boat was spent curled up on a sofa in the lounge, still clutching the orchid in its box that David had given me.

The train to Victoria was packed but I persuaded the steward to let me travel in the restaurant car while I had breakfast. Never had food tasted so good! I'd had nothing since leaving Hamburg apart from some coffee that an English army family shared with me – I had no more German money left.

From Victoria I crossed to Euston and arrived at the studio in Birmingham by midday. I was late, of course, but Tony Shryane was very understanding and I was still able to record my scenes.

When David joined the company in Kiel he was in the corps de ballet and not only danced in the ballets themselves but also when needed in the operas and musical comedies. After a time we had a telegram, saying 'Half-solo contract', which meant that he might dance minor solo roles but could still be called on to do operas and musical comedies. Finally, it was 'Solo contract'. No more operas or musical comedies, he told us jubilantly, but he loved opera and would enjoy them from the auditorium.

One day, when David was in his teens, he told me that what he wanted in life was to be married with a family and 'to be like you and Dad.' It was the nicest compliment he could possibly have paid us, I thought, however it led him to marrying much too early. When he was 19 he fell in love with the daughter of one of the opera singers in the Kiel State Company. We all felt they were too young and that she was not so committed to settling down as David, but you cannot forbid young people and alienate them – you can only stand by and pick up the pieces if things go wrong.

Roger had fewer misgivings and in the absence of the bride's father, gave them a lovely wedding in our church in England. Her mother, grandmother and cousins all came over and Ros was a bridesmaid. At the back of the church was a row of David's ex-girlfriends, all wearing deepest black!

Back in Germany, and with David working in the theatre at night the young wife soon reverted to her previous, carefree lifestyle and David realised he had made a mistake. At 21, they were divorced. He moved to another state theatre and there he met a young English dancer, who later told me that the moment she saw David she decided he was the man she would marry. She helped him get over his divorce and eventually he told me one day: 'I'm thinking of asking Deb to marry me.' 'I don't think you could do better,' was my reply.

It was a relief that this time he would have a charming English girl not only as a wife, but as the perfect dancing partner as well. To see them in pas de deux was the most beautiful thing, a joy to Roger and me. They had good careers too as they moved from company to company, becoming soloists.

The day of the wedding of Prince Charles and the late Lady Diana, 29 July 1981, *The Archers* were working in the studio. We were given a TV in the Green Room so that those of us who were not in the studio could watch between scenes.

I drove home, knowing David and Deborah were staying and that Ros would be at home as well. On arrival, feeling tired, I found three more members of the State Ballet Company of Braunschweig there as well: Edgardo and Paz, a delightful couple, were in one bedroom, David and Deb in another, my mother in her room while Roger and I were in the fourth. Ros immediately volunteered to sleep in the summerhouse and Leslie, another dancer from the company, was bedded down on the settee in the living room – what you might call a full house!

I am constantly amazed and sometimes appalled at the way members of the present Royal Family are depicted by actors in films and TV. To me, it all seems wrong and sometimes the parodies are libellous.

It was a wonderful day when an ecstatic David phoned from Germany, saying, 'Listen!' In the background was the lusty cry of a newborn baby. His daughter, our grandchild, had arrived. It was the long summer break at the theatre where he and his wife danced so when Claire was three weeks old they drove over and stayed with us until David had to return for the new season. Deborah and Claire stayed on and I found myself looking after a tiny baby for the first time while Deborah went up to town to train and get into shape again, ready to resume her career. Before he left, David showed me how to mix Claire's feed – he was always so wonderful with her. Roger too was immensely proud, as numerous snapshots testify.

David and Deborah were then working in Braunschweig and had a nice home with a lovely garden. They spent part of the long annual holidays with us; part with Deborah's family and another part in our holiday home in Menorca. A dancer's life is hard: ballet is the highest form of athleticism and by the time David was 36, he was experiencing serious back trouble.

Then came the fateful ballet that virtually ended his career. It was a Gershwin evening of three one-act ballets. David had a character role in the second and in the third one, *Rhapsody In Blue*, his role included a pas de deux. As a result of the difficult choreography in that ballet the principal male soloist sustained a back injury, which meant that he was unable to dance. David, as next in seniority, had to take on his roles as well as his own.

We were there and saw the final performance. David danced in the first modern-style ballet, his own character role, in the second ballet and in addition to his own role in the third ballet performed the big pas de deux. It was exquisitely done but the taxing lift of the ballerina, prone from ground level, damaged David's back as well. He managed to complete the season but realised he could no longer carry on. Later, he had an operation on his spine but suffered recurring pain for the rest of his life.

His wife, a beautiful dancer, was naturally not ready to retire. Their partnership had been such a joy to watch, they were so beautiful. So of course she needed a new partner and she soon fell in love with the young dancer who replaced David. Their marriage broke up and within a few short months, David lost his career, the wife who he told me many years later had been the love of his life, the little daughter he adored and of course, his home.

That was when he began to drink heavily and he battled against it without success for the rest of his life. We were able to follow Claire's progress until the marriage ended and she and her mother moved to Austria. I see her less frequently now since she and Deborah emigrated to Australia but she is a beautiful girl, artistic and creative. She didn't want to be a dancer but frequently works backstage in a Sydney theatre, where she is able to use her creative talents.

Many years later David tried marriage just once more. This time it was with a neurotic girl who of course couldn't cope with his drinking and it lasted only months.

A year or so before his death David was admitted to hospital with severe stomach pains. Pancreatitis was diagnosed and he was warned that another drink could kill him – alcohol destroys the cells of the pancreas. Needless to say, it didn't stop him drinking: he was out of control.

When he came home for the last time he told me: 'I shall probably die before you, Mum.' I was too shocked and upset to ask him more and ever since I have felt that I failed him when perhaps he wanted to unburden himself to me. Sadly, there are always regrets. We had previously talked about him coming back to live in England but the sympathetic treatment he received in Germany and the hospital facilities for coping with his addiction were so excellent that we both agreed it was better for him to stay there.

Now we spoke on the phone frequently. Sometimes all he was able to say was: 'Sorry, Mum.' Sometimes he was hallucinating and I could only tell him I loved him and that I prayed for him. I thought of him last thing at night and first thing when I woke in the morning – it is a sorrow you live with all the time.

He then decided that he was not going into hospital ever again, that he would cope with his illness himself. I rang him and he sounded sober but weak. He told me: 'I haven't had a drink for 36 hours and I'm suffering for it.' I said that he knew he shouldn't stop suddenly without medical help – he had told me how dangerous it was – but he insisted: 'I've got so far and I'm going to see it through.' He sounded calm and determined and I told him how proud I was of him. The last thing he said to me was 'Love you.'

The next day he didn't answer the phone. He had died during the night of 2 November 2006 of a massive internal haemorrhage: the alcohol finally breached the wall of his pancreas.

David wasn't a social binge drinker – he drank alone out of unhappiness – but for whatever reason anyone drinks to excess, they are slowly killing themselves. It fills me with despair to hear of young people binge drinking. I want to shout: 'Look what it did to our beautiful, talented, funny and loving son and stop before it's too late!' If they can't control it in the early stages it will end up controlling them.

David was cremated in Germany. Ros and her partner drove to Nuremberg: 'I'll bring him home to you, Mum,' she said. Now he lies in our beautiful churchyard near to Roger.

• Chapter 18 •
Travels and Treasures

I am not widely travelled but I've seen quite a lot of Europe. An invalid mother and the war kept me at home until my late twenties.

After Roger's time in India and Burma his peacetime job provided him with a good deal of foreign travel, which he professed not to enjoy. I did, however, get a trip to Amsterdam with him and with the wife of a colleague visited Anne Frank's house. That afternoon we saw the film *Cabaret*, which seemed very apt.

So, Roger wasn't keen to add pleasure trips abroad to his itinerary. We did have two enjoyable trips to Paris while my parents looked after the children, though, and then of course there were the family holidays in Brittany and the Balearics. Once David went to Germany we followed his progress with visits to Kiel, Kassel and then Wiesbaden, a beautiful city with a magnificent theatre. At the premiere of a ballet we were all in full evening dress and to stroll about in those palatial surroundings during the interval was like living in a dream.

It was a tradition to drink Sekt (sparking wine) in the interval which meant – at least as far as I was concerned – trying to stifle the burps for the rest of the performance!

After Wiesbaden came Munich, Augsburg and finally, Braunschweig, where David's career ended. He was there for some years and I came to know it quite well. At the instigation of an old friend he eventually moved to Nuremburg but unfortunately the friendship seemed to fizzle out almost as soon as David got there. Soon his only friends were fellow sufferers that he met during sojourns in hospital – one was a great support to him.

Nuremburg too is a beautiful city and I got to know it well, but I could never bear to go back there – it is too full of memories of my many visits to David. I have one golden memory of a beautiful summer's day when he took me to the zoo. Their marvellous tram system (which always runs on time to the second) transported us all the way to the outskirts and stopped at the zoo entrance. The animals are all in outdoor enclosures amid pleasant surroundings. We ended at the outdoor cafe with a large ice cream each.

As I couldn't persuade Roger to go abroad with me and he was still quite fit so he could be left alone, I took Ros instead. For her eighteenth birthday we visited Paris. Each day we took the Métro to a different area and then walked to see the sights – by far the best way of seeing the city – though at a later date Helen and I went together to celebrate umpteen years of friendship. On that occasion we did it the lazy way, both of us having been unwell, and chose a package deal.

When it came to Montmartre I said: 'You don't want to go in Sacré Coeur – I know where there's a cafe just round the corner in the Place du Tertre where they have gorgeous cream cakes.' I can't think how I kept so slim in those days!

As Roger said he'd rather stay at home, Ros accompanied me again, this time to Florence and Venice. We did all the tourist things – Michelangelo's *David*, the Uffizi, the marvellous view of Florence from the hill – a photographer's dream. There was a replica of *David* near our hotel and I embarrassed Ros by remarking: 'Hasn't he got a beautiful bottom?'

We arrived in Venice by train and as we emerged from the station I stood still and just laughed. I thought, It's just like a great big film set! It was such a surprise to be confronted by canals and gondolas outside a station. When we got back to England we watched *A Room with a View* and after that, and seeing all my photos of Florence, Roger said: 'I wouldn't mind seeing Florence.' Now he tells me, I thought, but I set about booking a trip to Florence for the two of us the following year.

It was not a success – our hotel was not the central one that Ros and I had stayed in, but half a mile from the centre. Roger had stupidly come in a brand new pair of shoes and the weather at first was hot. He suffered and it didn't help when he tripped on a high curb – he spent the afternoon in our hotel room while I went to suss out the buses and taxis. On my way back, I too tripped on a high curb and grazed both knees, though I was wearing trousers. Roger's comment was 'Bloody Florence!'

We went to San Gimignano, where it was cold and wet and a mist obscured the view. I must say they make a heavenly wine there, though, which we drank back at the hotel.

I have a photo of Roger in his mac sitting on a bench while waiting for a church to open and exchanging looks of hatred with a pigeon. The caption for that picture is 'Bloody Florence'. It was the last time we went anywhere abroad together apart from our home in Menorca.

After that Ros and I travelled to Lucerne. My father had been there with a friend in 1912. They went over by boat and train, of course, with an overnight stay in Paris, where he said they were too tired to do anything but go to bed. I wanted to see it because he had been there. I can't imagine it has changed at all in the old area. My idea of heaven is to take the paddleboat on the lake to Vitznau and sit outside the cafe with that wonderful view of the lake and mountains.

Before we went, Ros told me: 'Dad said, "I can't think why your mother wants to go to Switzerland. It would be much cheaper to go to France!"' I was just as amused as Ros. Following this, there were no more trips abroad as I could not safely leave Roger, but after his death I decided that I had better resume my travels while I still could.

First came a wonderful tour of Andalucia, which included the glorious Alhambra. I made a good friend on that tour and we still exchange news. After that I became hooked on river trips: the Seine, the Rhône and the Douro. Then I diverged and went to a floating town on the Norwegian fjords but I'm reverting to the river again for the Rhine.

While on a River Douro cruise we were taken to Salamanca, where the Plaza Mayor must be the most beautiful square in the world. How lucky I have been to see such beautiful places.

They say that one of the most traumatic experiences is to have a burglary. The sight of all one's most intimate possessions tipped over the floor and the sense of violation, that some stranger has been in your home, can make you feel it will never be the same again. While on holiday just after my 90th birthday I was burgled, but I was spared most of that upset.

My daughter met me at the airport on my return. Ros took my hand and said: 'I've some bad news, Mum.' My immediate thought was, Oh no, someone's died, so when she told me that I'd had a burglary the relief was tremendous. I had only lost things – not someone I was fond of!

When I arrived home it all looked normal for everything had been tidied away. Ros even apologised for not putting things back in the right place! How lucky I am to have such a daughter. All the silver was gone – all our wedding presents.

Ironically it had just been cleaned so it was looking its best for the great day!

I had given some of my jewellery away and just kept the things that had special memories and associations for me. My engagement ring, the brooch Roger bought me to celebrate my OBE, the ring that I had bought to console myself for being 40 – oh well, I'd had it for 50 years! All the other sentimental pieces too were all gone.

Anyone planning to pay me a nefarious visit would do well not to bother – I haven't replaced anything and I'm not going to! It's all in my memories and that is enough. My burglar still hasn't been caught and despite being able to produce photographs, nothing has been found. Some people have been burgled several times, so I suppose I can count myself lucky.

I was asked the other day what I collected, to which I replied: 'Plastic bags.' Not little ones but the sort you get when you buy clothes: stout ones with handles, much too good to throw away. I don't think that was what they meant, though!

To me what's worth collecting are the little things that remind me of someone special or a memorable occasion: in other words, souvenirs. Some bring pleasure, others poignant memories – I have some of both. On my bedside table is a Burmese cowbell. It stands for the years when Roger and I were apart during the war. He found it in the jungle – just the top of it showing above the mud – and he thought that it might be a Japanese booby trap. Being an engineer, and also foolhardy, he scraped away the earth until he uncovered it and brought it home as a souvenir. Had it been a booby trap as he suspected, I might have been widowed much sooner!

These days I often use a stick and one I use and treasure belonged to my father. It has a horn handle with a silver filigree band round it. I don't know what the wood is but it was obviously a young man's fashion accessory, possibly a 21st birthday present. My mother also used it in her last years and now it helps me round the shops. I feel that my father, having always been my rock, is still supporting me.

When the burglar came he took everything he thought was of value, but he left me the one piece of jewellery that mattered more than any of the others. It is a little marcasite brooch in a cheap plastic box and the gift card is still with it. In laboured, very childish writing, it says: 'To Mummy with love from David'. That, together with a lock of silky golden hair, is one of my most poignant souvenirs.

Over the years, Ros in her generosity has given me many beautiful gifts that I treasure, but loveliest of all is a gift card that says: 'To thank you for putting up with me for seventeen years and to say I love you'. The difficulties of the teenage years are wiped away in an instant with such a loving message. She gave me another wonderful souvenir on my 90th birthday in the form of an album of photographs of my whole life, so beautifully presented it represented many hours of meticulous work. It deserves to be a family treasure.

On the little table by my chair in the living room I keep a letter-opener given to me by my one-time helper and dear friend Nora. I use it every day of my life. Though I do not need to be reminded of her for she is often in my thoughts, her affection and thoughtfulness give me pleasure anew each time I use it.

Of my dear friend Helen I have a poignant reminder. When she was terribly ill in hospital and near to death she still remembered my birthday. I still have the card she wrote, obviously with great difficulty, with her love and birthday greetings.

Another of my souvenirs is in the house in Menorca. In a drawer by my bedside is the tiny collar and lead worn by my beloved cat Pickles, who died much too young and is so greatly missed. Are we masochists that we keep souvenirs which more often than not bring tears to the eyes?

Working in radio can involve a good deal of sitting around in the Green Room while waiting for one's scenes to come up.

Everyone has their favourite way of passing the time and crossword puzzles have always been a favourite.

When I was involved in big productions – Saturday Night Theatre or Wednesday matinees, for example – there was even more time to fill. *The Times* crossword was a favourite with male members of the cast and more often than not, we women brought our embroidery or knitting with us. Marjorie Westbury was a great knitter and a piece of graffiti once appeared on a screen in the studio. It said: 'Marjorie Westbury will not die – she will just unravel'.

Dear Marjorie! I wonder if she did . . .

Gwen Berryman, our Doris Archer, was an embroiderer and some of us have tray cloths she did to remind us of her warm personality. I too embroidered an afternoon tea cloth and napkins; I also did a tapestry that ended up so distorted that I hid it in a drawer for 25 years! Then one day I discovered a picture framer who steamed and shaped tapestries so now it graces my hearth as a very nice fire screen.

These days I do the Codeword Puzzles and enjoy the chat that goes on. Tim Bentinck (David Archer) does the Saturday *Telegraph* General Knowledge one but most of that is beyond me, as are the laptops which some members of the cast bring along to catch up on other work.

I think it's rather sad that emails are taking over from letter writing. It may be quicker and more efficient, but I know which I would rather receive. A handwritten letter brings the writer right into the room – besides, I like writing letters. Think what a treasury of letters from the past, giving us such insight into the life and times of famous people, would have been lost if all they had written was emails.

When I moved to London, leaving my dear friend Helen behind in Nottingham, we wrote to each other frequently. I had so much to tell her and I couldn't get it down fast enough. She said reading my letters made her breathless!

A source of great pleasure to me is the little Thai girl I sponsor. I heard about the organisation Compassion through my church and an offer of sponsorship brought me Ploy. She was then nine years old and belonged to a poor family. Through Compassion and her local church she is watched over in her schoolwork, health and moral guidance and protected from drugs and prostitution.

We have exchanged letters and photographs for four years now – they have to be translated, of course – but she is beginning to write a few words in English. Here is a typical letter from her:

Dear Granny June,

May God bless you and family. Thank you for a letter and a birthday card that you made for me Auntie Ros. I like it so much. Please give my regard and thank to her. I'm so happy that you like my picture. I hope you have a beautiful garden with lots of flowers. I like all kind of flowers because it is so beautiful. I would plant flower if I have a land. I was planted a bergamot in a pot. However it was not grow up because of a small pot.

Please pray for my Sunday School class because I couldn't remember a Bible verses. I wish I could remember Bible verse. May God bless you with a good health.

Love in Christ,

Ploy

I treasure the drawings she does for me. Always there are gardens full of flowers, and Ploy and Granny June holding hands with the caption: 'Ploy love Granny June'. There is always a cat or two in the picture – she knows the things I like!

The young actor who plays Peggy's grandson Tom, Tom Graham, sponsors a little boy in Africa and he went out to meet the little chap. I don't suppose I shall ever meet Ploy for she lives far up-country in Thailand and the journey would be more than

I could manage, but I hope the loving bond that has grown between us will encourage her in life. Ros has assured me that she will keep the sponsorship going when I am no longer able to. Sponsoring a child growing up in difficult surroundings is something I can thoroughly recommend to everyone.

For anyone wishing to find out more the address is: Compassion UK, 43 High Street, Weybridge, Surrey KT13 8BB.

Chapter 19

Work, Ros and Parties

In the 67 years that I have been broadcasting, I have seen many changes. When I began working in the Midland Studios in 1943 they were situated on two floors above a car showroom. There were four studios: the one on the first floor I associate with *Through the Garden Gate*, a Children's Hour fantasy programme with songs.

In those days of live broadcasts we were able to leave as soon as we had finished, even before the programme ended. We would have a taxi waiting at the door: as each actor finished they would dash down into it and while the credits were going out at five to six, we would be off in time to catch the six o'clock train to London!

With the traffic and one-way systems of today we certainly couldn't do that now. Studio two on the second floor was for plays, feature programmes and later *The Archers*; studio three was a talks studio and the big studio four was for music of all kinds and programmes with an audience, such as our Children's Hour pantomimes.

I remember going into the ladies' room once and hearing a little bleat from a holdall on the floor. Liz Marlowe, the original Lilian, had brought her tiny kid because it had to be fed every so often and she couldn't leave it at home!

The artistes' Green Room for studio two was very tiny and with seven or so actors in there, it was perfect for catching other's colds, which is why we nicknamed it the 'Breeding Pen'.

After we moved into our brand new state-of-the-art radio and television studios at Pebble Mill in 1971 we were able to spread ourselves. We had a large space in which to relax between scenes, a club and two canteens. Being conveniently close to Canon Hill Park, we could take advantage of walks enjoying the flowers and lake during our breaks. As I enjoyed rowing I took a boat out one day. The man in the kiosk looked at me in surprise: 'On your own?' he asked. 'Yes,' I replied, 'haven't you heard of Super Gran?'

When it was decided that we should move back into the city centre in 2004 Pebble Mill was razed to the ground. At the time I said 'This place will see me out', but each time I go to the new studios now I pass the overgrown site and in my mind I go up the steps where Arnold and I received all the visitors to the Archers Convention, each of them photographed with 'Jack and Peggy'. I walk along the corridor and turn left into the studios and the Green Room, where I was given a surprise party after getting my OBE and another to celebrate my eightieth birthday.

If I go back in my mind to the smaller of the two canteens I pass the place where I was once 'laid out dead' in *Doctors* and more cheerily, if my memory takes me up to the big canteen, I remember standing on a chair to watch Princess Anne arriving by helicopter at the police sports ground when she came to formally open Pebble Mill. It is like a ghost haunting a building in reverse: in my mind, I have been walking through the ghost of a building. Inevitably the move to the Mailbox was a bit confusing at first, but we soon settled in.

We were greatly saddened by the death at this time of chief sound engineer Mark Decker, who had been on the control panel for so long and of whom we were all very fond. There is a plaque to his memory on the wall of our studio.

Many of you will be members of Archers Addicts, but for those readers who do not know about it, I will enlighten you. Anyone who is a fan of *The Archers* should join. Membership means you are sent a quarterly newspaper to which you can contribute your opinions and letters. You hear all about the characters and behind-the-scenes doings of the actors with news and photographs; you can also buy items specially associated with the programme and get special terms on cruises and other occasions where you can meet the actors – and every year you get to vote in the SAMMY Awards. Named after Peggy's car. There are numerous categaries for example: What was the worst storyline? Which character tugged at your heart-strings?

The Archers has given me many friends – too many to mention them all, but to name but a few: Paddy Greene, Jill, whom we all love; Ted Kelsey, with whom I worked long before he joined us as Joe Grundy – a kinder, more thoughtful man you couldn't wish to meet; Brian Hewlett, Neal, who shares my love of Menorca and has a great knowledge and love of bird-watching; Charles Collingwood who keeps us all amused in the Green Room with his hilarious anecdotes and his sweet wife Judy, who plays Shula.

I sometimes wonder if the listeners ever think of what lies behind the characters we play? The parallel lives of June and Peggy must inevitably spill one into the other. My experiences of life are all grist to the feelings and emotions of the character I play. I am by nature an upbeat person. My glass is always half-full, not half-empty, and this has carried me through many difficult periods of my life; my faith in God is also an enormous source of strength to me.

Another great joy has been the little girl we adopted. Cute little Ros, with her big brown eyes, always knew what she wanted to do. From a very early age I noticed how good she was with visiting children and babies. For her out-of-school project she chose to help in a centre for disabled children and she applied to *Blue Peter* to join the 'Riding for Disabled Children' scheme. She didn't think to ask me first, but I was happy to ferry her there in her special uniform!

It was not at all surprising later on when she wanted to make the care of children her career and she trained at Ewell Technical College. Ros cares passionately about the welfare of children and has worked with babies through to teenagers. She may be small (just 4ft 11in), but through her voice alone she can put the fear of God into stroppy teenagers, even in the face of being threatened with a broken bottle.

Several times she spent her leave in Romania, working in a nursery that gave the orphanage children a few hours each day of cleanliness and love. She became very fond of one poor little soul and I treasure a photograph of them together. When she heard that the girl had died she dropped everything and flew out for the funeral, taking with her nice clothes for the child to be buried in. She told me: 'They were not new, but they were clean. They bury them in rags and that's not right.' At least the poor waif knew Ros's love in her sad, all-too-short life.

For several years she offered respite care to various children with complex autism through a contract with the local county council and she now works for a local Sure Start Children's Centre as a playworker for the under-fives.

Being old and rather deaf I have finally resorted to hearing aids. Having pushed one of them into my ear rather too enthusiastically, the end bit came off and was embedded in my ear. As ever, Ros came to my aid and took me to the local hospital, where it was removed. More than once she has had to take children to the A & E when they stuffed things into their ears and as she remarked, 'I didn't expect to have to take my mother after getting things stuck in *her* ears!'

She has always been there for me when I needed help.

It had been apparent to me for many years that Ros was not going to make a conventional marriage. When in middle age she fell in love, it was with an equally kind and caring woman. Although traditionally not a conventional union, they complement and care for each other and it is a joy for me to see their happiness in each other. I was pleased to join them at their Civil Partnership ceremony in September 2007.

So, I don't have a son-in-law but another, very welcome daughter and our affection is mutual. Her name is also Ros, so they identify themselves to me as 'Big' and 'Little'. Big is almost a foot taller than my little Ros. They are so public-spirited and when they moved to Suffolk quickly became known as caring and helpful members of the community – I'm so proud of them. Big Ros's parents, Eric and Joan, have become my good friends so I have been doubly blessed.

For my eighty-ninth birthday Ros and her partner took me out for a surprise dinner. I didn't know where I was going and the big and delightful surprise was the inclusion of my favourite goddaughter Susan and her husband Howard. This gave the girls the inspiration for something far bigger for my ninetieth. They immediately began a year-long plan of 'borrowing' my address book and, completely unbeknown to me, they contacted almost everyone in it. I say 'almost' because some of the names are no longer of this world.

After the event, I found that letters and emails had been flying all over the world for a year. People I saw every day, people I worked with, my hairdresser (a listening centre for the whole village) . . . everyone knew there was to be a big party – except me. I came to hear how tricky it had been at times for neighbours and people I'd spent holidays with – how hard it had sometimes been not to give me an inkling.

In the meantime, everyone on the programme, I learned, had also been trying to organise something on my birthday, which also happened to be an *Archers'* recording day. Unwittingly, I threw a spanner in their works by announcing well in advance that I wanted that day off as I was planning a little celebration for a few friends at home: I was planning to hold it in the garden with a buffet lunch.

I asked my friend Jody, who is never happier than when cooking for hundreds, if she would help with the catering. She willingly agreed – without telling me, of course, that she would also be catering for the big party the following week. It was a beautiful hot summer's day and my birthday was everything I could have wished for. The girls and I went to church at 9am, where the whole congregation sang 'Happy Birthday'. On my answerphone was the whole cast of *The Archers* singing 'Happy Birthday' and the following day I went to the studios, where I was given a huge bouquet.

I knew the girls were going to take me out for a 'cream tea' – somewhere nice, they said, so the following Saturday I put on my best summer dress and they arrived to take me out. Although they didn't seem in any great hurry to leave, eventually we set off in the direction of Leatherhead. They then took all sorts of devious turns and didn't seem to know where they were going. I knew later that they were just killing time. Finally, they said: 'We'd like to put a little bandage over your eyes.' I said: 'You can't do that because of mascara' – I didn't want to arrive wherever we were going looking like a giant panda! So we compromised and I kept my eyes tight shut. Eventually we stopped, by which time I was convinced we'd arrived at the local golf club, where I'd once had tea before.

They led me out and Ros said: 'There's a little step.' 'Too late,' I said. Finally, they told me: 'Open your eyes.'

Talk about gob-smacked! In front of me were over 100 people from all walks of my life and of all ages. There were cousins I hadn't seen for years (one from Canada), old friends, people from the church, past and present, a large contingent of *The Archers* led by Vanessa Whitburn, Graham Gauld (who'd come all the way from Aldeburgh), friends from Scotland, David's dearest friend Andrew, the son of an old Nottingham boyfriend, Helen's son, goddaughters and sons, Gillian Reynolds from the *Telegraph* . . . For a few moments, I could not have said a word to save my life. There were photographs and two cakes to be cut – I'd had about five altogether. How blessed I was with such daughters and such friends.

Big Ros's parents, who had moved house from Ireland to Solihull only five days before, had left all their unpacking to drive down and work tirelessly getting the hall ready. It wasn't until I walked out at the end that I realised to my surprise that I wasn't at the Golf Club, but a local village hall two miles from home. That just goes to show how gob-smacked I was – and I never did get my cream tea!

Epilogue

I had a phone call one day that left me literally gasping. It was to tell me that the Lord Mayor of London proposed to award me the Freedom of the City of London. How could such an honour come my way? After hanging up, my immediate reaction was sheer disbelief. Some joker must be pulling my leg, I thought, and I wouldn't allow myself to believe it until the official letter confirming it arrived.

In jocular fashion, I was told that even if I borrowed some sheep from David or Brian I would not be allowed to drive them across Westminster Bridge – apparently that archaic privilege is no longer part of the package. In fact, I have just one sheep, given to me by Hedli Nicklaus for my ninetieth birthday. I call her Baa-bara and she straddles the arm of my chair and I love her. Perhaps I will take her to London one day to make up for the disappointment!

So, on a perfect summer's day in June 2010 came the occasion that was something like a fairy tale: I was to attend the Guildhall in London to be made a Freeman of the City of London. This called for a special outfit and I had a long search before I found something suitable. A pretty voile skirt and a silky jacket in my favourite blue seemed to fit the bill, then a hat. I remembered the trouble Peggy had in finding a suitable hat for her wedding to Jack. The modern hats are so huge that I look rather like a mushroom under one of them, so I settled on a fascinator – a mad choice for an old lady, I suppose, but I think I got away with it. Roger would have laughed it to scorn, I'm sure, but I think David would have approved.

I was told that I could bring a limited number of guests, but with so many friends it was not easy to choose a representative few. Having settled that, I ordered a people carrier to transport the local contingent and me up to London. The rest of the party would assemble at the Guildhall, including Rozzy and Ros, *Archers*' editor Vanessa Whitburn, my goddaughter Susan and her husband Howard, nephew Nicholas and his wife Solveig from Roger's side of the family, my friend and publisher Jeremy Robson and Donald Steel from the BBC.

How I wished Roger and David could have been there too, but perhaps they were with us in spirit. We were introduced to the various dignitaries and finally, the Lord Mayor himself and the Lady Mayoress arrived.

At 12 noon we were ushered into the Chamberlain's Court, where I was told to advance to the Bench – rather like a judge's bench – where the Clerk of the Court handed me the Declaration of a Freeman which I read aloud. I promised to be true to the Queen, obedient to the Mayor, to keep the peace and warn the Mayor if I heard of any conspiracies against the Queen's Peace. That done, I signed the Declaration Book and was given a framed Copy of the Freedom and the book of Rules for the Conduct of Life; I was then offered 'the right hand of fellowship' and greeted as a Citizen of London.

We were then entertained by a talk from the Clerk about the background and history of the Freedom, which goes back to the fourteenth century. There were interesting tales of famous recipients, including Florence Nightingale – who he knew I had once played! He had certainly done his research.

He had made a display of *The Archers'* souvenirs, one of which was of the old 'Bull' beer mats signed by Denis Folwell – Peggy's first Jack – to which I added my signature. He had a Peggy Archer's cookbook (nothing to do with me!) and we were also reminded that the late George Hart (Jethroe Larkin) was also a Freeman but a grade above me for he had been a silversmith and thus a liveryman. It seems the Lord Mayor, the Clerk of the Chamberlain's Court and many others at Guildhall are all keen *Archers'* fans.

The ceremony had been very impressive and although it was made clear to me that it was not an Honour (an Honorary Freeman is for more exalted people such as Lord Nelson and Winston Churchill), I could not help but feel greatly honoured to be made a Freeman of our great city. The presence of the Lord Mayor and Lady Mayoress made the occasion all the more special – it had been the Lord Mayor's wish to mark the 60th anniversary of *The Archers* and my being the only remaining member of the original cast led him to offer me the Freedom.

I in turn presented the Lord Mayor with a framed front page of an *Archers'* script signed by members of the cast, which seemed to please him greatly. Lots of photographs were taken and we were offered a glass of champagne. The Lord Mayor then had to take his leave of us to carry out other engagements of the day.

We were given a short tour of other historic rooms of the Guildhall and in the Great Banqueting Hall it was interesting to see Gog and Magog at last. It was also a happy surprise to see a huge painting of an auspicious occasion featuring the Queen and many other members of the Royal Family. As soon as I noticed it, I remarked that it looked three-dimensional, as if the figures stood out from the canvas. It was painted by the artist David Poole, who for many years had lived just across the lane from us at home in Surrey.

We then moved into an adjoining room, where we were given a delicious celebratory lunch. Having just made a solemn declaration that I would 'keep the Queen's Peace in my own Person' I was careful not to over-indulge in the wines! In a final and charming gesture I was given the beautiful flowers that formed the centrepiece of the huge table, around which 20 of us had been seated. I also have a copy of the splendid menu signed by everyone there. It was truly an amazing experience and far exceeded my already-high expectations.

Later that evening I took two yellow roses from the flowers they gave me. One was for Roger's grave, the other for David's. Then at last I felt they had shared my day.

Being an only child taught me self-reliance even in spite of my shyness, so I grew up a bit of a loner, preferring to be with a few friends rather than one of the crowd. Sometimes I may be thought to be 'standoffish' – I'm the one who sits quietly in a corner, a listener rather than a participant, but not missing anything. And when I make a friend, it is a friend for life. Sadly old friends die off, but I believe we should never stop making new ones. My greatest delight is to take one or two friends to Menorca, those I can relax with without having to entertain them all the time – I'm so lucky in having a good number of them.

When life comes up with the hard knocks we have a choice: either we go down and give up, or in the words of the song, 'Pick yourself up, dust yourself down and start all over again'. In the process of coping with my share of life's adversities I've become very resilient. When I tried to encourage him to cope with his drink problem, David used to say: 'Oh, Mum – you never give up!' I would reply: 'That's my motto – never give up.' Remember Winston Churchill! That resilience is something I have in common with Peggy: one of her grandsons once remarked, 'Gran's a tough old bird!' – and so am I.

I was so lucky to have come into radio before the popularity of television took hold of our lives. Work was plentiful and varied – a good role in a classic serial could mean one or two days' work each week for up to 10 weeks. 'Live' programmes meant returning each week to Broadcasting or Bush House for rehearsal and transmission. The rest of the week might be filled with feature programmes, Children's Hour or Schools Programmes – I think I learned more from the latter than I did from many a lesson at school!

It is good to hear that radio programmes are gaining listeners again – in cars and on iPods, whatever they may be. Television entertainment is somehow losing some of its appeal, except for sporting programmes. I love watching tennis and snooker on TV – you could not get such a close-up view of the action if you were actually there at the venue.

I have never yearned to see my name in lights. Such ambition that I have had has been to work towards being a good actress and I'm still learning. From the start, I made up my mind that I would not forward my career by way of the casting couch and I have kept to that, perhaps as much from pride as morality. If so, I admit to the failing of pride. As I have already said, I've never had an agent. Having decided to make radio my field, I've been lucky enough to be constantly employed by recommendation alone for 67 years so I must be doing something right! I think I made the right decision all those years ago when Roger was coming home.

I loved the theatre passionately, but I have come to love radio equally. The knowledge that we are reaching out to so many people, conveying the thoughts and emotions of the characters we play, touching the hearts and minds of our listeners through our voices alone is such a fulfilling feeling. I'm often asked if I think of retiring. As long as the BBC wants me and I can get to the studio, I shall carry on. If I start to fluff my lines, miss cues or otherwise be a nuisance rather than an asset then that will be another matter and I hope I will bow out gracefully – it hasn't happened yet!

For me, the greatest reward is the approval and praise of my fellow actors and directors – and that I have received in recent years from those wonderfully generous friends and colleagues in *The Archers*. Bless them all! So here I am a nonogenarian, still doing the work I love. I have my dear daughters and so many good friends among the cast, in the village where I live and on the lovely island of Menorca – and I wouldn't have had all that without *The Archers*.

My life has not been lived on a grand scale and I've done nothing spectacular but coped with each day as it came. I had loving parents, a good husband and was entrusted with the lives of two young children, who have fully returned the love I have had for them. Thankfully, I still have one of them: my dear Ros. In writing my story, I set out to amuse rather than edify – or heaven forbid, to shock, as so many autobiographies seem to aspire to. I hope that I have made you smile, perhaps raised a few laughs – I laughed a lot as I was writing it, except for the bits that I wrote through tears.

Thank you for joining me in this ramble through my life. See you in Ambridge!

Monologues

Here is one of my 'odes and oddities':

The Tale of Oswald Croaker

This is the tale of Oswald Croaker
Who lost his clothing at strip poker.
He said, 'I can't go home all bare,
I'd catch my death in this cold air.'
So struck a newspaper with gum
Around the middle of his tum,
And round his shoulders and his back
He draped the Club House Union Jack,
And with his bowler on his head
He left the club with stately tread.
But ere much progress he could make,
A crowd assembled in his wake,
And noting Oswald's bright array
They said, 'It must be empire day,'
And striking up 'God Save the King'
They gathered round him in a ring,
And Oswald's Union Jack unfurled
As up into the air it whirled.
The poor man, trying not to wilt,
Clung grimly to his paper kilt
While someone read the racing tips

Displayed on Oswald's papered hips,
And a small boy cried, 'Look Mum,
He's got a cartoon near his thumb!'
The ladies favoured Oswald's thighs
Which told them how to make mince pies,
While pencils jabbed him in the rear
Where the crossword puzzles did appear.
But Oswald really seethed with rage
When someone tried to turn a page,
And rushing through them like a gale
He caught the paper on a nail
Which left him with a bowler hat,
(And you can't hide very much with that).
Next day before the Magistrate
Stood Oswald listening to his fate.
The charge was really rather stupid,
'Twas 'Posing in the Park as Cupid'.

Below is an excerpt from one of my American monologues:

Entertaining the Vicar's Wife

'Oh, good afternoon dear Mrs Stitch. Do sit down; you've called about a Sale of Work? Well now what do you know about that! I never knew the unemployment trouble was that bad. Fancy having to sell work! I must tell Elmer. Elmer's my husband, you know, and he's so generous I'm sure he'd give the poor people some of his work. He works for the Cough Free cough manufacturers in Colorado – "One dose and you'll never cough again". He has such a sweet blonde girl to help him. They visit all the big drug stores in London – and it sets my mind at rest because I know she looks after him like a sister. And they do work! Do you know they sometimes don't finish till three or four in the morning, and when Elmer gets home he's that tired he can't stand up properly or talk sense or anything. He says his doctor's ordered him to take whiskey to keep his strength up.

'And how's the dear, cute vicar, Mrs Twitch-Stitch? You don't allow him to go gadding about with blonde hussies? No, I should think not indeed! I know I wouldn't if I were you . . . Just look at him at that last Mother's Meeting!

'And how are the little stitches, Mrs Stitch? You've only got one! Of course, how silly of me! A stitch in time saves nine! Ha, ha – er – yes, yes.

'Of course you've met my Junior? Yes, he is a playful little fellow, and so clever! Too clever? Oh, do you really think so? That reminds me, it's time he came to bed . . . he's out playing in the garden . . . [she goes to window] Junior! Oh Jun-i-or! . . . Oh if that's my umbrella, bring it at once! . . . It isn't? It only belongs to that old . . .? Oh, it's only yours, Mrs Stitch! . . . Now then, Junior, come to Momma! Bedtime! Yes, Junior, yes! YES! Right away! . . . That's right, never mind what Momma said last night . . . These children! How they do imagine things . . . Poor Mrs Stitch can't help being like that, can you Mrs Stitch? No-o. And Junior, don't pull such faces at the kind lady. Why not? Because your face might stay like it and then they won't have you for a film star! Oh, now don't cry, Junior. Yes! . . . It's because he's too tired . . . he's usually so obedient! Well, Momma'll tell you just a teeny-weeny bedtime story first. Now what shall it be about? The Three Bears? And by the Three Bears, Junior, I do not mean the three strip-tease girls. No, Junior, I will not tell you a Little Audrey story – no, or about Mae West.

'Why not? Why, because – er – because – er, Mrs Stitch has heard them all before! She wouldn't want to hear them all again! What's that, Mrs Stitch? You most certainly have not heard them? Well, now, just fancy! And your husband told me such a naughty one the other day! You know . . . Junior, if you'll go to bed now I'll buy a box of candy . . . Well, then, two boxes of candy . . . Yes, Junior, Yes, and a water pistol! Oh . . . Mrs Stitch

The Alzheimer's Research Trust
www.alzheimers-research.org.uk

Alzheimer's Society
http://alzheimers.org.uk